To Luke & Cha

Romans 1:19-ino 1135

[signature]

Plain View

By Tom Rawls

Published in association with Awesome House Productions

Copyright © 2016 Bobby Thomas Rawls

ISBN: - 978-1-326-74155-6

All rights reserved. No part of this publication may be reproduced or transmitted in any form or by any means, electronic or mechanical including photocopying, recording or any information storage or retrieval system, without prior permission in writing from the author.

The rights of Bobby Thomas Rawls (also known as Tom Rawls) to be identified as the author of this work has been asserted by him in accordance with the copyright, Design and Patents Act of 1988

Unless otherwise stated, all scripture quotations are taken from the Holy Bible, New International Version. Copyright © 1954, 1958, 1962, 1965, 1987 by the Lockman Foundation

MSG - The Message Copyright © 1993, 1994, 1995, 1996, 2000, 2001, 2002, by Eugene H. Peterson

NKJV - The Holy Bible, New King James Version Copyright © 1982 by Thomas Nelson Inc.

KJV - The Holy Bible, King James Version Public domain

Cover photo taken by Tom Rawls as graffiti art in the city of Milan, Italy. It is public domain.

Cover art created by Liz Morgan

Interior layout by Mr Tim Handley

Dedicated to my wife Denise:

Thank you for your love and support for me, our family and our ministry together. You are gorgeous with a beautiful spirit. You've been such a great companion in life, partner in crime and overall fun person. I look forward to growing old together with you by my side.

Like Proverbs says, "Who so findeth a wife findeth and good thing and favour in the eyes of the Lord!" I'm so glad I found you! I am eternally grateful our world's collided! I am a better man because of you.

All my love to you – forever.

What are people saying about Tom Rawls and Relentless?

Brian Houston, Global Founder and Senior Pastor of Hillsong Church. Tom's broad life-experiences, coupled with his service to the Church have given him a unique perspective and understanding. I believe those who venture into these pages will see the Church from a more vibrant perspective - as profoundly powerful and vastly underestimated.

Craig Groeschel, Senior Pastor of *LifeChurch.tv*, Tom Rawls' passion for the local Church and all that it can accomplish is inspiring.

Mal Fletcher, Chairman of 2020Plus, social commentator, broadcaster, futurist and author. In Relentless, Tom Rawls gives us a compelling vision of the majestic force Christ's Church might become, if she is willing to re-align herself with the revolutionary principles of the New Testament. His call for leadership... and spiritual potency... must not fall on deaf ears if Western Church is to once more become Christ's 'city on a hill'.

Dave Gilpin, Senior Pastor of Hope City Church, England and author of a runaway seller *Sacred Cows Make Great BBQs*. 'Relentless' has always been the tattoo etched into the heart of Tom Rawls. He has never relinquished, never quit, never backed down and never stopped. This book is infectious. You may become what you read.

Wayne Alcorn, President of the Australian Christian Churches and Senior Pastor of Brisbane City Church, Australia. Tom Rawls is a pioneer. He's been used by God to provoke thought and action. [H]e has retained a freshness in his approach to leadership, a passion to stay in touch with culture and a prophetic edge to his message. This book captures his understanding of current trends, and his heart to see the Church be the unstoppable force its founder meant it to be.

Gary Clarke, Lead Pastor Hillsong London. Tom is articulate and challenging in his approach. He brings a fresh voice and a new perspective as he unwraps well-worn passages of scripture. His passion for the church is infectious."

Endorsements for "Plain View"

I have known Tom Rawls for over thirty years and in that time all I have known is a minister who lived on the edge, and accomplished great things while there! The concept of this book reflects how Tom thinks. This book is on the edge, relevant, contemporary and a must read! **Dr Scott Wilson, President of Eurolead.net Network, Author, Church Consultant, International Speaker, Leadership Coach**

Tom Rawls gives us an insightful look into how the 21st Century church can *'re-introduce'* Jesus to this generation 'in a way that they can relate.' Like the men of Issachar who 'understood the times' Tom is a man who understands 'these times.' *'Plain View,'* is reminder of the fact that Jesus continues to reveal Himself clearly to every generation, and often in places we may least expect. If you are passionate about reaching the people in 'your world' then this book will be a powerful tool to help you do just that. **Paul & Deb Hilton, Country Directors for AOG World Relief, Vietnam, Cross Cultural workers in Asia.**

Plain View is a brave project. Tom decided to put his years of ministry experience and insights into plain view. Dripping with blood, sweat, and tears, the words on the pages of this work will definitely cause you to stop and consider your times, your culture and your tribe from another vantage point. The heart of God beats in this work and it will quicken the heart of any reader who is ready for it. It's in plain view but you need to recognize it! **Patricia DeWitt, Life-coach, Artist, living and working in Paris, France.**

'I've known Tom for 40 years and during that time Tom has consistently distinguished himself as a leader and preacher 'in touch' with contemporary culture. Working in a mission's context myself, I understand the importance of being contextually relevant and of speaking the 'language' of the people with whom we're seeking to communicate. Tom does this brilliantly. In his book *Plain View,* Tom captures and conveys the importance of these with great insight, a sound Scriptural perspective and a unique understanding of the influences on culture. I highly recommend this book for every preacher who wants to connect with people. **Bruce Hills, International Director, World Outreach International.**

Contents Page

Preface: Dateline

Part One: On the Edge of Glory
Chapter 1: White Blank Page
Chapter 2: Tripping the Hardwire of the Human Heart
Chapter 3: Secular Prophets

Part Two: Re-presenting Jesus Christ to a Waiting World
Chapter 4: The Deity of Christ
Chapter 5: The Humanity of Jesus
Chapter 6: The Death & Resurrection of Christ: a Dramatic Adaptation for the Big Screen

Part Three: The Ascended Christ - Apocalypse RIGHT NOW!
Chapter 7: John on Patmos - Not the Jesus I thought I Knew!
Chapter 8: The Ascended Christ - Radical Beyond Measure
Chapter 9: Audacious - Big - Bold - Potent - Wild - Jesus on Display

Part Four: Never before seen footage of Jesus Christ
Chapter 10: Living in the Question - Jesus Christ Superstar
Chapter 11: Avatar - Longing for Something Better
Chapter 12: Angels and Demons - The Hunt for Truth
Chapter 13: Star Trek - the Human Heart's Yearn for Adventure
Chapter 14: The Book of Eli - Jesus and the End of the World
Chapter 15: The Twilight Phenomena... What the heck is going on?
Chapter 16: Gladiator - The Cry of the Human Heart to Fight
Chapter 17: The Walking Dead – Search for Purpose and Meaning
Chapter 18: Downton Abbey – A Desire for a Better Life

Part Five: Elvis Sightings - Seeing Jesus in Remarkable Places
Chapter 19: Conclusions

Acknowledgements

Jesus Christ: Hiding in Plain View

Preface: Dateline

Christianity will go. It will vanish and shrink. I needn't argue with that; I'm right and I will be proved right. We're more popular than Jesus now; I don't know which will go first - rock and roll or Christianity. **John Lennon (1940 –1980) of the Beatles.**

Today people pick and choose what they believe about Jesus without accepting His full identity. They craft a god in their own image to meet their needs, and then they stick the Jesus label on their idol. **J. Lee Grady.[1]**

Dateline:

16th September 2010
Edinburgh, Scotland, United Kingdom

A tsunami of secularism[2] crashed on the shoreline of a relentless Church[3]. It changed everything irrevocably. Corresponding with Pope Benedict XVI visit to Edinburgh, an aggressive strain of secularism made a bold and public stand. Throughout the United Kingdom there were public protests and significant media coverage.

2016 – Terror Worldwide

From suicide bombings and mass murder in the Middle East to young girls being kidnapped and raped in Nigeria. From car bombs massacring 100's in Iraq to women and children murdered in cold blood by a runaway truck in Nice, France.

---

[1] J. Lee Grady is contributing editor for *Charisma*. He was the magazine's editor for 11 years. He has been involved in Christian journalism since 1981.

[2] Secularism: the separation of religion from state affairs. 'Secular' refers to the removal of Biblical moral values, Christian ethics and the very belief in God from what a nation should act like and move as. What this term means is that secularists wish to have no point of reference with God or the Bible.

[3] Relentless: A Renaissance Theology for the twenty first century Church written by Tom Rawls – Available on Amazon

From wars in Syria to the biggest migration of humanity in decades. From shootings in Orlando to shooting in Paris. From an attempted coup in Turkey to a failed state in Libya. From gay people being thrown from buildings to their death by Islamic extremists to scores of men lined up on the shores opposite Europe and being beheaded.

From journalists being hacked to death in Bangladesh to Baton Rouge where police officers are killed by a sniper. From Brexit to the most bizarre election cycles the world have ever witnessed. The world around seems on the verge of a meltdown, divided and confused.

Something frightening and scary is happening all around us.

My Premise: Is it possible that the spiritual climate of the Western world has realigned? Is the spiritual climate signalling a profound change for our foreseeable future? Will we look back in history and surmise that it was this moment that heralded the inauguration of a pre-Christian culture in the Western world?

For decades now, social commentators and Christian leaders have said we live in a "post –Christian" climate, but is that an accurate assessment right now? Has culture shifted even more significantly? More importantly, was the shift significant enough for the Church to even take notice?

My question is: Has this major shift in popular culture signalled a return to a "pre-Christian" world view? If the answer is a "yes", then does the Church need some recalibrations? If the Church is aware of this massive change, has she altered course in an attempt to more effectively communicate Christ?

It's no surprise that we now live in a generation where many have no knowledge of Jesus Christ. The Church of Jesus is ignored and discounted by many. The world around stands unimpressed with our antics and communication.

Plain View

If this is **anywhere near the truth**, has the Church been made aware? Are there appropriate adjustments going on? Has today's world view been contextualised by the Church for the 3rd Millennium Church to more effectively communicate Jesus Christ?

Is the Church in the West ready or even equipped to communicate in this multifaceted and complex climate? Will the Church "cut it" doing what we're doing now or will we need to make further changes to facilitate a more effective communication of Christ? How do we do this? What communication strategies do we need to employ?

In the midst of this aggressive secularism, humanism and atheism I believe and am convinced of this one thing; that **this is our finest hour as a relentless Church to lustre like a "city on a hill"**[4]. Keep in mind; it was in the **exact cultural conditions** that the early Church saw such great success and ultimate expansion.

In the first century no one had heard of Jesus Christ and yet the Church literally exploded in size and influence. The first century world was in profound spiritual darkness and drowning in the ocean of hundreds of religions with a thousand personal variations and, not to forget, the ubiquitous supreme worship of an Emperor who thought he was a god. Yet Christianity exploded to the four corners of the Earth in less than a hundred years. Within three hundred years it would touch every aspect of the world and its major cultures.

Could this happen again... in our day? I think the answer is a rousing and resounding YES! For this reason I am supremely excited. The New Living Translation of **Habakkuk 3:2** says, *"I have heard all about you, LORD. I am filled with awe by your amazing works. In this time of our deep need, help us again as you did in years gone by. And in your anger, remember your mercy."*

---

[4]Matthew 5:14

I believe that the 21st century will be known in the annals of Church history as our greatest days. It will be a time when the Church will unveil and reveal a stunning, astonishing and irresistible Christ for the entire world to see. Jesus will be seen in all of His beauty. His presentation so enthralling as to quench the thirst of this spiritually parched generation.

Jesus will be communicated as the Christ potent in power, the Christ strong and so compelling. He will once again startle the world with His ability and capacity. He is mighty to save; to save an individual, to save a household and to save a generation. In truth there is no other name under Heaven where by men can be saved.

As the Church *we are certainly not alone* in our desire to re-present Jesus Christ to a world truly ignorant of Him and His claims. Before Jesus ascended back into Heaven, He assured us "I am with you always, even until the end of the world."[5] We can be assured that the creative and resourceful person of the Holy Spirit is with us and has gone before us like a foreign correspondent.

It is my firmly held belief that the Holy Spirit has embedded Himself into various aspects of culture, education, art, humanities and society. He waits to assist us to unearth Jesus Christ and reveal Him to a waiting world hungry and thirsty for reality, power and a sense of the eternal.

Jesus Christ is not hidden from this world - He is in plain view and He is simply irresistible – radical beyond measure. It is our joy to communicate Him to an unbelieving world and make Him known.

Adele's number one international hit says these words, "Hello, can you hear me? I'm in California dreaming about who we used to be.[6]"

---

[5] Matthew 28:20

[6] Adele co-wrote the song with her producer, Greg Kurstin.

Could it be that the Spirit of Christ is speaking, calling out to a broken and thirsty world? I think so!

I genuinely hope you enjoy this book. Make sure you encourage others to read it and work with these powerful principles.

Sincerely,

Tom Rawls
Norwich, England. October 2016.

tomrawls@proclaimers.com
www.twitter.com/tomrawls
www.tomrawls.com

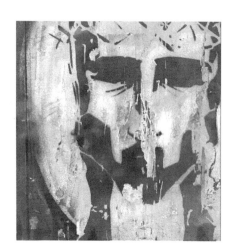

Part One: On the Edge of Glory

Love is an irresistible desire to be irresistibly desired. **Robert Frost.**

Your beauty trumped my doubt. **Mumford and Sons, from their song "Winter Winds".**

Beauty awakens the soul to act. **Dante Alighieri, 13th century Italian poet.**

You are beautiful beyond description, too marvellous for words, too wonderful for comprehension. Who can grasp Your infinite wisdom who can fathom the depths of Your love, You are beautiful beyond description, Majesty, enthroned above. **Mark Altrogge.**

Chapter 1: White Blank Page

I was born in the great nation of America - "home of the brave and the land of the free!"[7] My world was a generous world with a national image of success, positivity and enthusiasm. I would say the Pledge of Allegiance to the flag every school day and we would sing the national anthem. I had a very strong and pronounced southern accent. I lived in a nation where liberty, freedom and the pursuit of happiness were God given rights to every citizen. We prayed every morning for our nation.

At the age of eleven my family and I moved to Australia - "the Great Southland of the Holy Spirit."[8] The cultural contrast, though not empirically observable by me as an eleven year old, was, none the less, a powerful divergence. The impact of the cultural shift was not lost on me as a pre-teen! I became a second culture kid. Suffice it to say, ***Australia was very different from America!***

As I grew in my understanding I found Australia was a relaxed and friendly nation. Everyone said, "G'day" and it was meant as a

---

[7] January 28th 1957.
[8] Pedro Fernández de Quirós, (1565–1614) was a Portuguese navigator who named the continent of Australia.

greeting. Everyone was a "mate" and you needed to be "fair dinkum!" The kids in my school didn't say "yes ma'am" and they didn't wear shoes either![9] The national song was about a homeless man who stole a sheep and rather than be arrested he commits suicide in a pond of water!

The beginnings of Australia and the beginnings of the US could not have been more different; one established to celebrate religious freedoms the other as a penal colony for petty criminals. As a second culture kid I began to see, assimilate and compare and contrast this second culture with my first. I purposely developed a strong Aussie accent too because I needed to fit in.

Then remarkably at the age of thirty four there was another move afoot! I moved with my wife and family to Bangkok, Thailand. The contrasts again was staggering. Thailand, or Siam, had been a nation for thousands of years. I saw the ruined city of Ayutthaya which was established a thousand years before James Cook discovered Australia and Columbus discovered America!

Thailand had a unique and difficult language very different from English (or even American!). This nation of exotic customs and mysterious traditions was simply mind blowing. But we learned the language well enough to publicly communicate and we learned the culture well enough to be accepted as only an outsider ever could be.

In 2003 yet another move took me and my family to the United Kingdom; more in a moment. But these moves were all important to the development of my experience in communicating Christ cross-culturally.

A convert:

---

[9] In 1967, primary school kids living on the Gold Coast usually didn't wear shoes - it was so warm!

There was another set of experiences which are noteworthy: I was converted to Christianity at the age of seventeen and a half. I was godless before this experience and was consumed by the pagan culture around me. I had never really read the Bible, hadn't been to a church since I was seven years old with my grandma back in the States and I was theologically ignorant and biblically illiterate. The night I was converted was a powerful night when I had a vision of Christ and it was His potent beauty that trumped my doubt!

As a consequence of being a convert at seventeen, I was not a person soaked in the Church culture of the sixties and seventies. Add to this the fact that there were thirty other kids of my age who also made a decision to follow Christ almost all at the same time. This mini revival in the local church had a profound impact on the way we did church life and how we followed Jesus.

We were all counter-culture people with a "hippy" mind-set. We had all smoked cannabis - and yes we did inhale[10]! Thankfully there were some wise pastors and leaders in the church who had the ability to break down the complex biblical themes into everyday language that we as young teenagers could understand. They broke it down and brought us from known to unknown and did it so powerfully; leading us to discipleship.

Let me share a bit more of my journey! I entered ministry after 3 years in Bible College at the tender age of twenty one. As a communicator I was always seeking to make people listen to the Bible by using a number of tactics. The one I employed most was the shock tactic that made people sit up and either "get it" or get offended. I didn't mean for them to be offended but must say I really underestimated the power and the entrenched nature of Church culture. I also sought to use humour to get people to laugh where I could smack home the truth without breaking teeth or splitting lips. Some laughed - others didn't.

---

[10] Thank you Mr. Clinton!

My church in Melbourne started in 1984 and lead by me until early 1991; it is a case study maybe for another book! Early in the piece a young couple joined our church - Dave & Rosanna Palmer of the pub band "Rosanna's Raiders." It was a powerful departure from normal Church culture to have a rock 'n' roll band leading the services with a light show and smoke machine! Believe me, in mid 80s Australia this was radical!

One newspaper's headline read **"Rock & Rawls has them in the aisles!"** One dissident who left our church around this time - an older couple in their seventies went to another church and the local pastor greeted them at the door and asked where they were from. Their answer was revealing; "We've come from that Tom Rawls' church - it's a circus down there and Rawls is the chief clown!" Amusing, right? But hey, it was 1984!

In our Melbourne based church, we attracted a load of people not normally found in Church at that time in Australia. We had street kids, drug takers and pushers, metal heads (oh did I mention we were also the home church for the metal band Mortification?![11]) as well as a church full of young people with wild clothes, dyed hair and piercings. It was a fun radical atmosphere - always exciting!

Steve Rowe, lead singer of a heavy metal band[12], asked me one day if his band could play one Sunday night at church. I hesitated a little; but then he said he could get 300 of his Melbourne fans to attend. I told him if they played 3 songs and then he introduced me as his pastor it was goer! He agreed, we did it and the rest is history! Melbourne was my first experience of speaking about Christ to an emerging generation who had a pre-Christian mind-set.

After Melbourne, I spent twelve years in Thailand in an environment where Jesus was **totally unknown** to the masses. I was well and truly

---

[11] http://en.wikipedia.org/wiki/Mortification_%28band%29
[12] http://roweproductions.com/

on my way to being a cross-cultural agent and had honed my communication skills down quite well.

During this time I travelled extensively in and around Asia; in countries like Laos, Cambodia, Vietnam and Myanmar. I spent three years working in Dhaka Bangladesh, a predominately Muslim mega city very different from Buddhist mega city of Bangkok.

I knew now how to use existing culture to become my launch pad into biblical truth. I knew how to use folk stories, local customs and specialty foods to communicate the good news about Jesus. I had learned to leverage the elements of culture like music, local celebrity and media to become quite expert in communicating Christ in a generation that had never known Him. I was able to use language as well using slang and dialects to get a message across. We were seeing some great success.

Common Grace
It was around this time I was introduced to the concept of "common grace." I had, of course, heard of it before from my Bible College days but had no idea really what it was and how it really worked. I was amazed to see that the concept was in scripture and this theology was articulated and powerfully employed by many... including God Himself.

But more about that a little later....

As a cross-cultural agent, I was convinced that God had not forsaken ancient or modern culture but had put significant sign posts into every culture and tongue. As a good missionary, I had read *"Eternity in their Hearts"* by Don Richardson.[13]

I knew God had plans for every culture and in every generation. I believed that God's word was relevant and could be communicated

---

[13] Available from www.amazon.com

in many ways to speak powerfully to any generation and culture no matter how complex they were.

I believed that God, by the agency of the Holy Spirit, had gone before the Church in every nation and had prepared a place for us to take unbelievers through a process that employed "common grace" to intentionally lead them to "special grace" and a revelation of Jesus Christ and His salvation.

It was my view that Jesus Christ was present in every age and actually hiding in plain view. Today's society and culture lies literally on the edge of glory; waiting to be revealed.

United Kingdom:
On my arrival in the UK in 2003 I was now embarking on my 4th culture; it was second nature by now. I worked intuitively in my 4th culture. As different as America was to Australia the UK was *a whole other culture* with its own peculiarities and cultural idiosyncrasies as well. Just having a white face and speaking English did not help me or help the Brits in understanding what I had been through, had experienced and had practiced.

I had moved to sleepy Norfolk; agricultural, rural and comfortable. Having been a world traveller I sought to once again to be an agent of cultural change. I embarked on the mission of becoming a cultural architect.

My vision was to reach unchurched people – I was tired of seeing a reshuffling of sheep from one church to another – I was sick of the Christian concept of shopping for another church that would meet my need. I was hungry to see people freshly connect with Jesus in an authentic setting we call Church. Just attracting people from other churches wouldn't cut it for me – I wanted to see the salvation of my city!

Early after I arrived in Norwich I began to see a load of university students come to Christ who were truly "London thinkers[14]" and they were fresh converts with loads of ideas. Being a developer of talent and destiny, I was in my element. I again sought to do what I did best and began to leverage popular culture in leading a generation to Christ *who had never opened a Bible, never touched a Bible, never read a Bible. Jesus was in plain view - I just needed some to help another generation see Him.*

These beautiful and intelligent young people had no experimental working knowledge of Jesus, they had no resident memories of Christ, no theology or working knowledge of structure of scripture and as pre-Christian they simply didn't know who Jesus was. I got to re-present Christ to them.

These kids had seen churches. They had grown up with the buildings just around the corner, they had visited churches for baptisms, weddings and funerals but regarded the business of church as BORING, dusty, meaningless and totally irrelevant to them and their everyday lives. We met a generation unimpressed with the thought of church. To them our Jesus was impotent, powerless, weak and inconsequential.

When we launched in the city of Norwich we labelled our church as "Church without the boring bits!" It captured the minds of a generation. Unfortunately, people who were from more traditional Church cultures couldn't get it; the phrase offended them and we got a load of criticism and some hate mail!

People inside my church were thrilled to see so many young people connecting with Jesus Christ! They were all in the change process of this new way of doing Church. I knew what I was doing - but there were a few who just never got it.

---

[14] These young people were not from Norfolk, they were from other big cities in the UK many of them from London - they just thought bigger.

We did all sorts of innovative things for the UK. We worked hard on creating an atmosphere the unchurched could connect with. We made sure that the songs we did in church were current and fresh; nothing over two years old was the guide line! Our language was simple and to the point, we avoided the use of "Christianese" opting to simply explain things in a language they could understand.

We elevated young people to positions of leadership quite rapidly and gave them a voice and a platform from which to communicate. This made a few of the older ones a bit annoyed and some got their noses out of joint. Most, however, recovered and became vital servants in the church; alas others didn't and moved on to other quieter and older churches with no babies, no teenagers and no young people.

We worked hard on our message series. I remember one of our now famous sermon series was entitled "Cult TV" where we sought to discover God's resonance in cult TV shows. We highlighted these TV shows to reveal that God had actually gone before us and was embedded like a foreign correspondent within these TV shows. We sought to show that Christ had not forsaken popular culture but on the contrary was standing in plain view!

We explained that if you just took some time, paused and **took a closer look** you could identify the DNA of God in these TV shows and could actually see His unique fingerprints all over popular culture. These young people, all in their early 20s, warmed to a language that was bereft of Christian terminology. We sought to communicate in a manner they could understand, we sought to create an atmosphere that would flick their 21st century switches and kindle the eternity already in their hearts. Far from abandoning popular culture we revealed a Jesus who was standing in plain view for all to see. In the words of Adele, "Hello, can you hear me?"

We intentionally used some of the top 40 hits from the radio as our pre-service and post-service foyer music. Some asked why we did this and our response was: "It takes a lot of courage for a person to come to church and if they at least recognised a song they would feel a little more at ease, perhaps thinking 'If they're playing Bruno Mars, Justin Bieber or Mumford and Sons these people mustn't be too bad!'"

Almost every year we did *Proclaimers goes to the Movies* and we'd seek to identify the "God particles" in modern media as well as identify the desires of the human heart. We would then show how God meets those needs through Jesus Christ. We made a deal of showing film clips and played popular songs to highlight God's presence in pop culture.[15]

I remember one Easter we performed the song, *Bleeding Love* by Leona Lewis.[16] Most people there didn't even know it was a Leona Lewis song and in the top 40 on the radio. "Sinners" heard it and were wrapped! Something powerful resonated in the hearts of our unchurched friends as they listened.

Redefining vocabulary
As a part of our journey we as a church sought to redefine Bible words like "repent" and "sinner." We sought to do away with trite Christian clichés and always sought to explain unfamiliar biblical language in the songs we used in church and messages we preached.

In an effort to deconstruct the traditional church service, we purposely tried to get rid of all the irrelevant parts and bring in as many fun aspects as we could. Most people understood what a "live event" was - a church service was a bit harder to sell. I know it upset the more religious – they were still very connected to "fire and brimstone" rhetoric. "Repent! The end is nigh!" But we had a generation to save and didn't have time to translate "Christianese."

---

[15] Most of our sermon series are on our website www.proclaimers.com
[16] http://www.youtube.com/watch?v=qaGINCdtJjU

As cross-cultural agents we sought to find the **secular prophets** of the day and give them a voice. Some found it really difficult to hear, for instance, a quote from Justin Timberlake, Rihanna or Lady Gaga. For others, more traditionally minded, the exercise was simply lost on them when we quoted Beyoncé or Clean Bandit.

I remember the day when one guy was so offended by me quoting Madonna that he left the church. The guy was a revival chaser and was upset I would access the comments of a person as immoral as that woman![17]

Study: Language Learning
To be effective as a cross-cultural agent we had to do some serious study. We actually had to learn the language of the day! Amazing hey - who'd have thought! Having learned Thai, learning 21st century speak was a breeze! We utilised technology and various aspects of modern media. It was such a creative time - and still is!

Some of our research involved going to see the latest releases of blockbuster movies. I loved that part. The other part was to understand the complexities of the music industry as well.

With so many young leaders we emphasised leadership development. We took advantage of that forum to re-educate the older more Church cultured people as well. We gave voice to a generation who were 21st century "insiders." Their message was authentic and potent.

We delighted in showing where God had gone before us to reveal the majesty of Jesus Christ. Many got it and were thrilled to now see Jesus in the most remarkable places.

We would have brain storming sessions to come up with great titles of new series, we sought the creativity of the Holy Spirit to recreate

---

[17] Check out the words of Jesus to the woman at the well in John 4.

Plain View

Church into a 21st century complexities of various cultures - all pre-Christian in orientation!

We discovered that salvation was a journey.[18] [19] We discovered how people travel as pre-Christians through to the point where they were able to actualise true repentance and find faith in Christ.

As a good missionary I was helping people come to an understanding of a God who "in His kindness takes us firmly by the hand and leads us into a radical life change."[20] My experience and my depth of cross-cultural understanding helped me and gave me the opportunity to mentor another generation to effectively communicate Jesus.

We continued to discover how to leverage pop culture and the secular prophets of our day to communicate Christ to a theologically illiterate generation without contradicting the message of the Bible.

We actively sought to observe the parallels with first century Christianity and dared to believe that we can see the same impact as the early Church leaders did, to become like those "men who **turned the world** upside down." [21]

Yes it is true this generation had little to work with in regards to theology and Bible knowledge but God made sure this generation had a rich mine field of divine intersections. It was our job to find those intersections and encourage a more thoughtful response. Jesus Christ takes great delight in standing in plain view actively encouraging us to find Him and seek Him out. This book is something of my story and my work book.

---

[18] http://www.angelfire.com/bc/normanhouseChurch/EngleScale.htm
[19] http://en.wikipedia.org/wiki/Engel_Scale
[20] Romans 2: 4
[21] Acts 17:6

True Pagans – Real Revival

People today are part of a pagan secular world; sexualized, sensuous, precocious and revolutionary. This doesn't mean they are not spiritual – every human being alive on the planet has eternity in their hearts. Our journey, our objective is to **trip the hardwiring** placed there by God Himself. We find we have the opportunity to re-present Jesus Christ to a generation in search of truth.

It is my deeply held belief that though the world around us today is deeply agnostic, atheistic and resistant to Christ we will see a move of God in these days that will rival the early days of Christianity; it will be a move of God many have dreamed about. We will be able to say, "This is revival!"

I believe that even now we are experiencing one of the most powerful moves of God ever seen in all of human history. We are on the cusp of a massive movement of people into the Church. It will be more powerful than any previous movement or recorded revival to date.

If what I see is any indication then something big, brash and shockingly spiritual is happening in the world around us and we need to stop and take a closer look.

I know that my way is not the only way. I'm not trying to be prescriptive. What I do want to do is prod people to reconsider their communication of Christ. I seek to inspire another generation in finding Jesus in a meaningful way we would call salvation.

Could it be possible that in this pre-Christian society we could see a revival more powerful than anything we have ever seen in all of history? I think the answer is YES and AMEN!

[Common grace] curbs the destructive power of sin, maintains in a measure the moral order of the universe, thus making an orderly life possible, distributes in varying degrees gifts and talents among men, promotes the development of science and art, and showers untold blessings upon the children of men **Louis Berkhof.**[22] [23]

When I began my career as a cosmologist some twenty years ago, I was a convinced atheist. I never in my wildest dreams imagined that one day I would be writing a book purporting to show that the central claims of Judeo-Christian theology are in fact true, that these claims are straightforward deductions of the laws of physics as we now understand them. I have been forced into these conclusions by the inexorable logic of my own special branch of physics.[24] **Frank Tipler, Professor of Mathematical Physics.**

Chapter 2: How to trip the Hardwiring of the Human Heart

Fra Angelico (c. 1395 – February 18, 1455), born Guido di Pietro, was an early Italian Renaissance painter, referred to in Vasari's "Lives of the Artists"[25] *as having "a rare and perfect talent". He was a Dominican friar in the monastery at Fiesole, Italy.*

His famous works were for Popes and aristocrats of the day where money was no object but he reserved his most outstanding paintings for audiences of one as he frescoed the cells of the monks in the monastery of the Dominican Brothers at San Marcos in Florence.

Fra Angelico communicated his deep reverence for Jesus and his knowledge and love of humanity on the bedroom walls of his beloved brothers. Each room was individually decorated and his art

---

[22] *Louis Berkhof* (1873 – 1957) was a Reformed systematic theologian whose written works have been influential in seminaries and Bible colleges around the world.

[23] Louis Berkhof, *Systematic Theology* 4th ed. (Grand Rapids: Eerdmans, 1979), pages 434-435.

[24] Tipler, F.J. 1994. *The Physics Of Immortality*. New York, Doubleday, Preface.

[25] Giorgio Vasari "Lives of the Artists" First published 1568: Penguin Classics, 1965.

inspired devotion and commitment to Jesus Christ and His plan on the Earth.

As is often the case, we communicate our best when we are far from the limelight and face to face with real people. Away from the constraints of wealthy clients and the limitations of panel painting, Fra Angelico was able to express his "... rare and perfect talent."

The Theology of Common Grace – Open Your Eyes and Take a Long Thoughtful Look
Romans 1: 19 – 20 says this in the Message translation, "The basic reality of God is plain enough. ***Open your eyes*** and there it is! By taking ***a long and thoughtful look*** at what God has created, people have always been able to see what their eyes as such can't see: eternal power, for instance, and the mystery of his divine being."(Emphasis added)

Open your eyes – take a long thoughtful look - He's standing in plain view!

Auto stereograms are 3D pictures standing in plain view. To see them you need to look in a different way than you would normally. It's the convergence of both focus and the angle of one's eyes. You look; you stare and then you see it! It's awesome to behold. A 3D image appears over a 2 dimensional picture.

Common grace is similar. You need to ***open your eyes and take a long thoughtful look***.

Pre-Christian
A pre-Christian spiritual climate does not mean people have NO religion or spiritual beliefs. On the contrary, you and I both know that man was created to worship; man was created to reach out to The Divine and The Unknown. We are hardwired for devotion. We were created worshippers and ***we will worship something or someone!***

Plain View

The book of Ecclesiastes in the Old Testament says that God has "***planted eternity*** into the hearts of men." The Amplified Bible brilliantly describes mankind as having ".... a divinely implanted sense of a purpose working through the ages which nothing under the sun but God alone can satisfy.[26]"

What we presuppose about a pre-Christian culture and climate is that apart from the Divine's [God] implantation of "eternity in their hearts," people have little to no pre-recorded data about Jesus. They don't know the Sunday School stories; they are ignorant of the Bible's famous characters, most have never read or even touched a Bible before. We presuppose they have no memories, experiences or pre-existing knowledge to even begin a biblical conversation; if we err it's a plus!

So the challenge is; how do you tell people about Jesus when they don't have a start point?

But wait – stop! The early Church faced this same problem; they lived in a sensuous world overly fascinated by sexual themes, inundated by countless religious forms and thoughts and overwhelmed by gods and goddesses of every shape and size! We see the same today. The shape of the god's have changed – the prophet's look a bit different – but we are in the same spiritual climate!

Missionaries for centuries have battled with this question in countless generations, countless countries, countless languages and countless cultures. I believe it is time for us in the Western world to battle with the same question of engaging a pre-Christian society.

---

[26] Ecclesiastes 3:11

Phil Cooke[27] tweeted "... in the UK we are not living in a post-Christian culture. We're in a *pre-Christian* culture!" I responded: "@PhilCooke[28] I have to say.... I agree."

It is my opinion that Europe is further along the road to a pre-Christian climate than is the US or even Australia; though some American sociologists may beg to differ I'm sure. Even though countries like Poland, France or Spain and ... even the US and the UK would consider themselves as "Christian" nations; most discerning people would disagree!

Europe is at the vanguard of the downward spiral of atheism, paganism and secularisation but I believe the rest of the West is not far behind. The rush to a pre-Christian world view is approaching fast and at a dizzy speed.

Stephen Fry, English comedian, actor, writer, presenter, and activist, spoke recently concerning his beliefs in God – he said, "Why should I respect a capricious, mean-minded, stupid God who creates a world that is so full of injustice and pain." A TV presenter asked him if God were real and he confronted Him, Her or It at the "pearly gates" what would you say. His response was "I'd say, bone cancer in children? What's that about?"[29]

Stephen Fry's comments resonate with many in pre-Christian Europe today. To so many in this age the message of the Church is, irrelevant, archaic and excessively boring; unable to touch their inner spirituality or meet their practical needs. They see an ancient Church, disabled by a "time warp" and immobilized by an "internal loop" system that continues to present a blurred, obscured and

---

[27] http://en.wikipedia.org/wiki/Phil_Cooke
[28] Twitter, August 2011.
[29] http://www.independent.co.uk/news/people/stephen-fry-responds-to-christian-backlash-after-confronting-god-with-bone-cancer-in-children-whats-that-about-10027984.html

untouchable image of Jesus Christ. If they do actually get a glimpse of Jesus they see Him as castrated, impotent and powerless.

Boring and irrelevant are words which immediately leap to their pre-Christian minds when confronted with the idea of "Church". They see a Church mired in an archaic and irrelevant morality unable and unwilling to tolerate the diversities of the 21st century. They see a Church unattached to today.

Common grace supposes that the knowledge of God is accessible to people through what God has created. The NIV translation of **Romans 1:20** goes like this: "For since the creation of the world God's invisible qualities his eternal power and divine nature have been clearly seen, being understood from what has been made, so that men are without excuse."

"Hello it's me!" Standing in plain view.
What Paul articulates is that from the beginning of creation people have had a deep and abiding "knowing" of the invisible qualities of God. From what has been made around them from mountain ranges to star constellations, from clouds full of rain to snow falling from the sky, from full moons to sunsets filling an evening sky, God's eternal power and divine nature has been seen.

This argument holds even more weight in the 21st century where scientific investigations into DNA, cosmology and nanotechnology has simply blown away some of the greatest minds in the world. Listen to a few in the field:

Alan Sandage[30] (winner of the Crawford prize in astronomy): "I find it quite improbable that such order came out of chaos. There has to be some organizing principle. God to me is a mystery but is the

---

[30] http://www.telegraph.co.uk/news/obituaries/science-obituaries/8150004/Allan-Sandage.html

explanation for the miracle of existence, why there is something instead of nothing."

Robert Jastrow[31] (1925–2008) was an American astronomer, physicist, cosmologist and self-proclaimed agnostic: "For the scientist who has lived by his faith in the power of reason, the story ends like a bad dream. He has scaled the mountains of ignorance; he is about to conquer the highest peak; as he pulls himself over the final rock, he is greeted by a band of theologians who have been sitting there for centuries."

Henry "Fritz" Schaefer[32] (Graham Perdue Professor of Chemistry and director of the Centre for Computational Quantum Chemistry at the University of Georgia): "The significance and joy in my science comes in those occasional moments of discovering something new and saying to myself, 'So that's how God did it.' My goal is to understand a little corner of God's plan."

So my question is, just *where* do you start to tell people about Jesus Christ when they have no pre-existing knowledge about Jesus Christ? How do you commence conversations with people who have no pre-recorded data about Jesus? Where do you even begin to talk about Jesus when the people we want to speak to have no memories, no experiences or touch points to start from?

I think common grace is the answer. People see, feel or experience something in nature that then trips the eternal part of them – I call it the "hardwiring" within them. Something flips the switch that leads their thoughts and imaginations back to God and His invisible qualities of eternal power and divine nature!

It is at these moments we need *to be there* to help explain and help them commence a journey of revelation.

---

[31] http://en.wikipedia.org/wiki/Robert_Jastrow
[32] http://en.wikipedia.org/wiki/Henry_F._Schaefer,_III

It's God's design in creation that has pre-prepared people for the supernatural and the hard to explain. I'm not proposing merely an ontological apologetic about God, but I am thoughtfully tapping into that eternality, that deep and supernatural emptiness inside each person which was actually created by God to know God.

Sun sets and Movie sets

So why just settle for a sunset when a movie set is so pertinent and close to hand? Not a huge leap!

Here's another question; could the Holy Spirit, whose chief work is to reveal Christ, be using the modern parables we call episodes of hit TV series to communicate to modern man? Is their very popularity evidence that something shockingly spiritual is taking place deep within their spiritual being?

Is it possible that the Holy Spirit is seeking to speak to the world through Hollywood movies? New York Times best sellers? Could it be possible that the Holy Spirit is communicating a message through some top 40 singles? Why settle? Adele's lyrics say, "Hello from the other side, I must have called a thousand times."

Here's my real point! Is it possible that God has not forsaken popular culture at all but is actually using it to speak to a generation about Himself? Is it possible that Jesus Christ has been standing in plain view waiting for us as cross-cultural communicators to tap into the 21st century mind?

Could it be possible that the Holy Spirit is reaching out to a generation who has forgotten God and is using "those things that are made"[33] as a hook to lead them to a powerful and life altering revelation of Jesus Christ? As a culture are we on the edge of glory revealed?

---

[33] Romans 1:20

Could it be possible that the Holy Spirit is using certain movies, books, songs and even some television adverts to "trip the hardwiring" (the eternity in our hearts) which in turn helps us start a conversation that would eventually lead to a full blown revelation of Jesus Christ?

This proposal, though clearly scriptural (I'll explain in a minute - keep the seat belt on just a while longer) is *not an easy place to navigate* for fundamentalist evangelical Christians; in fact it's quite difficult for those who are doctrinally well grounded and understand a systematic approach to scripture and truth.

Our dogmas; which are clear, concise and well-constructed make sense to us and are the superstructure for our faith. But our doctrinal constructs are at a bit of a loss with an existential generation who glut themselves on a panoply of sensual encounters and the impressive array of their emotional and palpitating experiences.

Can I suggest our theological constructs, *though true in every way*, may just no longer be *relevant or communicable* in 21st century communications? That's the constructs - not the actual theology. Don't read what I'm not saying.

As the Church, I purport, we need to search for *new touch points* and find those "triggers" that will nudge people towards spiritual curiosity. We need to search for and listen for those "secular prophets" whose words and actions trip the human hardwiring to connect with the divine; or at least start a search for it. We need to discover these prophets and give them voice.

Look a Little Closer
To answer these questions and more, we will need to "look a little closer." Learning to "look a little closer" takes time and patience. But those willing to engage with the 21st century's media saturated world with eyes and heart wide open in search of God may find themselves

Plain View

pleasantly surprise, spiritually energised and equipped to touch the lives of the people in our celebrity driven generation.

The meaning behind learning to **"look a little closer"** is the theological term **"common grace."** It begins with an appreciation of the creative side of God and the goodness initiated by Him from creation and continues on through the work of our conscience.

Common grace finds its first biblical roots in creation; where the heavens declare the glory of God. On the Hillsong album *A Beautiful Exchange*, there is a song called *Open my Eyes*[34] and it so aptly expresses this sentiment:

In the stars I see Your majesty displayed
In the heavens all Your wonders are proclaimed
I see Your fame in all of the earth
And I seek to know the ways of Your heart
Through the seas and open skies I hear Your praise
As the shout of all creation lifts Your Name
I hear Your praise in all of the earth
And I seek to know the ways of Your heart

Common grace operates wherever God used "questionable sources" to reveal Himself and call people to Himself and His truth.

There are many instances in the scriptures where God champions the concept of common grace such as when God used Cyrus, the Persian King to restore His people Israel[35]. Common grace is evidenced when God exhibits a sense of humour and playful surprise speaking through a donkey[36], a burning bush[37] and at one point even a witch![38]

---

[34] Hillsong Publishing – song written by Braden Lang and Reuben Morgan
[35] Isaiah 45
[36] Numbers 22: 28
[37] Exodus 3
[38] 1 Samuel 28

Jesus continues this unpredictable pattern when employing common grace:

- When He chose tax collectors and fishermen to initiate His kingdom.
- When He continually upset the religious of His day by befriending prostitutes; even allowing one to have free access to Him at a party so she could wash His feet with perfume and tears.
- When He defends a woman caught in adultery.
- He spends time explaining true worship to a woman who has had five husbands and lives de-facto with her current man.
- When, in His upside down kingdom, he spends time with social outcasts such as Samaritans, widows, orphans and even little kids and singling them out as particularly compelling role models to a highly educated religious audience.
- When He told rich people to sell their possessions and follow Him.
- When He healed on the Sabbath and called the religious rulers bad names!
- When His first miracle was turning water into wine to allow a party to continue for a few more days!
- When He healed a Roman centurion's servant when in fact Rome was the occupying power in Israel; he was not very popular that day!
- When His hero in one parable was a dirty, filthy mixed-race Samaritan man who helped a man beaten up by robbers. Come on now; in the Jewish mind of the day there was no such thing as a "good" Samaritan!

Common grace is not limited to merely the Bible texts that I have mention here or merely to creation as seen by the masses. Common grace is a much more powerful and pervasive vehicle than just that.

Common grace in action has been known to upset the religious and the conservative theologians amongst us; but we need to guard ourselves and our followers from this overreaction.

The encouragement is to learn to look a little closer; realising that there may be aspects of the subject which are useful and other aspects that are not helpful or useful and need to be discarded.

Common grace explains why the most spiritual movies, TV shows and popular songs are often made by people outside the formal borders of the Church but have the ability to trigger something spiritual in us. These producers, script writers and directors are our "secular prophets" even though they may look a little like donkeys!

Common grace explains why we are moved to tears during a movie, feel tingles when we listen to certain music and are moved to indignation when we watch see the actions of barbaric and uncivilised actions of ISIS and Boko Haran.

Common grace is seen in a song like *"Edge of Glory"* by Lady Gaga. Common grace can be seen in songs like *"Like a Virgin"* performed by preacher's kid and Catholic icon, Madonna. Common grace stirs a theme in the hearts of millennia's everywhere when they hear the lyrics of "Stay Awake" by Example.

In 2002, Madonna comments in an interview about her song "Like a Virgin." She says this; "At first, I was surprised with how people reacted to *Like a Virgin* because when I did the song I was singing about how something that made me feel a certain way – brand new and fresh. People thought I was saying I just wanted to have sex, **when it meant just the opposite**. It celebrated the idea of feeling untouched and pure. I like having the secret knowledge that what it said was good."[39] [40] (Emphasis added.)

Doubt if you must but she spoke directly into the hearts of millions of young women all over the world who had been the victims of

---

[39] Clerk, Carol (2002), *Madonnastyle*, Omnibus Press, page 41

[40] Rooksby, Rikky (2004), *The Complete Guide to the Music of Madonna*, Omnibus Press, page 17

sexual abuse, rape and those who may have succumbed to promiscuous sexual behaviour that left them feeling empty, hurt and worthless when it was all over.

How would the Church use this example of common grace? Maybe as a Christian communicator someone could have taken the opportunity to say something that flowed from her interview. Then take the time to sensitively yet confidently address the issues of sexual abuse, promiscuity and how people feel when they've been used.

Out of that discussion they may have launched into an explaining of what a relationship with Jesus Christ could look like. They could say that connecting with Jesus Christ can make you *feel brand new and fresh.*

2 Corinthians 5:17 says, "Therefore, if anyone is in Christ, he is a **new** creation; the old has gone, the **new** has come!" Connecting with Jesus can make you feel "untouched and pure!"

Can we see common grace at work with pop divas like Lady Gaga? (Don't lose me here! The best is yet to come!)

During an interview with Musicians@Google Present: "Google Goes Gaga"; she explains that *Edge of Glory* is "... one of the songs on the album that is truly one of my favourites, it's called *Edge of Glory* and it's kind of a sad story. But my grandpa died about five months ago, and my dad and I were going to say goodbye to him at the hospice, and later at my apartment ... my dad sat next to me at the piano and ... I wrote *Edge of Glory* on the piano and my dad and I cried. *The song's about your last moment on Earth, the moment of truth, the edge of glory is that moment right before you leave the Earth.* (Emphasis added.)

Plain View

On her Larry King interview[41], Lady Gaga said "I believe in Jesus, I believe in God, I'm very spiritual, I pray. At the same time there isn't one religion that doesn't hate or speak against or be prejudiced against another racial group or religious group or sexual group. I guess you could say I'm a very religious woman who is confused about religion."

Could this comment be a great place to start a conversation? A lot of people are confused about religion. A lot of people think the same as her in reference to Church. My question remains, is there an opportunity to reveal Jesus here?

As a matter of fact in my church we did the unthinkable and made a presentation of Jesus launching off her comments from the interview. Gaga made this comment about her latest album[42] she said it was about "... bad kids going to church, having fun on a high level."[43] Sounds a lot like my church!

When we take a closer look we are also being discriminate; not everything is useable. Some things we are able to discard and disregard. So don't misunderstand how to use common grace. I'm not silly enough to endorse everything Lady Gaga says or does!

Remember, there are rain clouds in some sunsets as well as litter on some mountain ranges; including dead bodies on mountains like Everest! Some sunsets look better than others and some mountain ranges are more inspirational than others. Madonna and Gaga created racy and sexually uninhibited videos but... *is there a strain of common grace coming out of them?*

---

[41] June 2010
[42] Born This Way (2011)
[43] MTV online magazine Dec 1 2010 9:42 AM EST - By Jocelyn Vena (@jocelyn1212)

This is why you need to take "a closer look." If God can speak through a donkey why can't he speak through a diva? (No disrespect to Gaga! #pawsuplittlemonster)

I know this is controversial! I know this is also upsetting for those who have a structured doctrinal foundation. Common grace is by its nature shocking, provocative and it undermines Christian preconceptions.

I remember, to one pastor's horror, when I mentioned *Buffy the Vampire Slayer* in one of my sermons. (... yeah I know, it was probably 11 years ago!) I was sort of laughed at and it was requested that next time I spoke in his church would I not speak about vampires! But *The Door* magazine once voted Buffy as *"theologian of the year."*[44] The article said "Indeed perilous times call for a bold theology." Is our 21st century society on the edge of glory?

In my church when we did the series called *Cult TV;* we took some cult TV shows and tried to show the resonance of Christ in them. It was a bit of "risky business" but it was a huge success! People started to "get it" and started to work out how to use the principles of common grace to start a conversation that would ultimately lead to a conversation about eternal issues. Imagine starting a conversation with someone about a TV show and ending up speaking about spirituality.

Now it staggers me why God uses who He uses! It is downright mystifying to me!! As a matter of fact why does He use these people anyway?? Madonna! Buffy!! Gaga? You've got to be joking!! The whole concept of common grace can at times be so subversive and, by its very nature, incredibly dissident.

So in the big scheme of things, why use a donkey to speak to a prophet? Why not use an Arabian purebred stallion? Why use an

---

[44] http://archives.wittenburgdoor.com/archives/buffy.html

animal at all - they don't normally speak, hey? Why use the witch of Endore to speak to a backslidden King? Why didn't God just speak to Saul in a vision, a dream or just come down and speak to him Himself?

Why did God decide to use CYRUS??!! (It's in capitals because I'm shouting.) He was a great leader, a good king and conqueror of the world but he certainly wasn't a believer in the God of Israel! He was far from being a man of good morals and godly virtue.[45]

Why did Jesus call fishermen, tax collectors and women of ill repute to help Him usher in His kingdom? Why spend so much time antagonising the religious rulers of His day? Why use despised Samaritans as heroes in His stories? Why speak to a serial adulteress and use her to spread His word to a city? Why did He heal a Roman centurion's servant knowing it would antagonise His generation?

But here is the character and personality of common grace: Common grace is subversive and dissident. Common grace allows God's goodness to fall on people who don't know Him and certainly don't deserve it. (**Maybe this is why it's called grace**.)

Common grace allows God to use whoever He wants to use to declare His grace and nature. (That's whoever He wants! **Maybe why it's called "common."**)

Common grace get a conversation started, it gets us connected to a person or an audience and common grace opens a door to the spiritual. It is special grace that leads to salvation.
It is "special grace" when we hear Billy Graham preach a gospel message! It is special grace when Reinhard Bonnke stand and say, "Africa shall be saved!" It is special grace when we listen to Taya Smith sing beautiful love songs to Jesus. It's special grace when we

---

[45] http://www.cyrusthegreat.net/

hear "Young & Free" singing "Real Love!" It's special grace when we hear our pastors preach and reveal the word of God on Sundays.

But it can only be common grace that explains why we feel so very deeply moved by a comment from Peter Petrelli (of *Heroes* fame) about "living extraordinary lives." It common grace when we hear Russell Crowe as Maximus saying "... what we do in life echoes in eternity!" It's common grace when we hear Christina Aguilera singing "say something I'm giving up on you." It's common grace when Ella Henderson sings "I keep going to the river to pray!" How roused were we when we heard Katniss Everdeen speaking as a leader to her people stirring their hearts for freedom?!

Common grace takes a bow when TV shows like *Blue Bloods and Madam Secretary* feature sincere heartfelt prayers to God. Common grace stirs us when we see shows where good overcomes evil.

Common grace moves me to tears when I watch a movie where I see a father turn and hug his son who is in need... and what he needs is just a big hug!

What I love about common grace is that it subverts and undermines the Christian's preconceived notions of **how, when and through whom** God can chose to communicate His divine truth. Common grace is dangerous, risky and at times precarious; and I love anything that undermines a good Christian preconception!

Common grace actually makes God bigger (if that is possible!) and lightens our load as communicator.

As we engage with our modern world it is common grace that encourages us to continue the search for today's burning bushes, talking donkeys and dishonest tax collectors.

The secular prophets of our age are just like the woman who had five husbands and wasn't married to the man she was living with!

Plain View

Common grace surprises us when we hear Gaga declares "Jesus is my virtue!" Or when Adele sings *"Hello, IT'S ME!!"* These are moments when common grace claims another platinum record and we continue to feel uncomfortable to find the most unlikely as God's instruments telling His message.

Common grace encourages us to take a closer look around us to see if there are any existing circuits in today's media to trip the God embedded hardwiring in humanity; especially a humanity with no pre-existing knowledge of God, Jesus and the Bible.

Common grace confirms what we all inherently sense; something big, brash and shockingly spiritual is happening in the world around us and we need to stop and "take a closer look."

Here's my point; God has never abandoned this world to an aggressive secularism, hiding somewhere in a galaxy far far away, but He has - through common grace - turned the table and He is speaking loudly and boldly to anyone who will listen!

In fact He is standing in plain view and He has employed His "rare and perfect talent" to paint pictures that are pure genius to anyone with a few minutes to spare.

"It is the glory of God to conceal a matter; to search out a matter is the glory of kings." **Proverbs 25:2**

Tom Rawls

The word 'common' in the title of the topic is not used in the sense that each particular favour is given to all without discrimination or distinction but rather in the sense that favours of varying kinds and degrees are bestowed upon this sin-cursed world, favours real in their character as expressions of the divine goodness but which are not in themselves and of themselves saving in their nature and effect. So the term 'common grace' should rather be defined as every favour of whatever kind or degree, falling short of salvation, which this undeserving and sin-cursed world enjoys at the hand of God. **John Murray[46] on Common Grace.**

I think faith informs almost every episode. I'm a skeptic who desperately wants some reason to believe. **Chris Carter, creator of the X-Files.[47]**

God writes the Gospel not in the Bible alone, but also on trees, and in the flowers and clouds and stars. **Martin Luther (1483-1546).**

Chapter 3: Secular Prophets

Michelangelo di Lodovico Buonarroti Simoni (1475-1564) was a Renaissance painter, sculptor, architect and poet. For the two years between 1498 and 1499, Michelangelo was engrossed in sculpting one of his most powerful and potent images of Christ called the *Pieta*. This sculpture depicted the crucified Christ dead and in the arms of His mother Mary.

The *Pieta* was carved from one piece of marble and is one of Michelangelo's most finished pieces of art. Michelangelo completed this piece of work when he was a mere 25 years old! He was a genius!

---

[46] John Murray (1898-1975), a native of Scotland, studied at Princeton Theological Seminary. He taught systematic theology at Westminster Theological Seminary from 1930 to 1966 and was an early trustee of the Banner of Truth.
[47] Craig Detweiler and Barry Taylor, (2003),*A Matrix of Meanings: Finding God in Pop Culture,* Baker Academic

Mary is depicted as incredibly young and youthful whilst the face of Christ is calm and lacks the signs of His great passion. Apart from the nail prints and the sword marks in his side, Jesus looks peaceful, tranquil and composed. His face is seen in absolute perfection.

But horror struck at 11:30am on the 23rd May 1972. The date will go down in the art world as tragedy! The *Pieta* statue suffered considerable damage when a mentally disturbed geologist named Laszlo Toth[48] walked into the chapel and attacked the sculpture with his geologist's hammer while shouting "I am Jesus Christ".

The statue was damaged, but not beyond repair. The nose of the Virgin was remade from pieces taken from the back of the statue and was consequently repaired. The face of Christ was not touched but ironically ***His hands and feet were badly damaged***. As a result of this attack, the *Pieta* is now protected behind bullet-proof acrylic glass to keep it safe from all future defacement.

As I think about this tragedy it seems that religious vandals have sought for generations to destroy the image of Christ; especially His hands and feet! The religious wreaked destruction through neglect and their self-indulgent, dusty traditions and have cheapened the visage of Jesus, damaging the Church.

Others seek to tie the hands of the Church and hobble her feet through their legalism. Some ironically have sought to protect the glory of Christ behind bullet proof glass, making Him untouchable, inaccessible and safe when in fact His desire is to be unfettered, unencumbered and totally unleashed into the world around us.

The world in the 21st century has changed dramatically. Most in society would simply ignore the Church. We are an unimpressive group to many. To many, Christ would appear castrated, impotent

---

[48] http://www.guardian.co.uk/notesandqueries/query/0,5753,-2565,00.html

and powerless. So how do we **re-present** Jesus Christ as relevant, potent and radical beyond measure?

In this pre-Christian culture, we will be allowed, in fact encouraged, to re-present the image of our Saviour using the 21st century as our canvas and stone.

Hebrews 2:9 says simply; "But we see Jesus....!" But do we? Do we see Jesus or our religion, our celebrity speaker or our favourite band? Are we presenting a Jesus people can relate to? How do we re-present Him to a waiting world? How do we communicate Him to a world desperately seeking after truth, reality and an authentic connection with the spiritual?

We are a generation fashioned by Darwin.

Many people today have no resident memories of Christ. Few were taught of Him as youths. Fewer still have an image to work from when we mention His name. The millennial generation has no operational images of Jesus Christ; there's no pre-existing data from which to form a workable image. As 21st century communicators, remarkably, we have a blank canvas. We have an incredible opportunity as never before.

Discovering the Secular Prophets: Paul in Athens

Paul, the writer of two thirds of the New Testament, was an amazing man of great intellect! He was articulate and relentless in his desire to make Jesus Christ famous. **Acts 17** finds him in Athens, about a week ahead of his team. Have you ever wondered what he was actually doing in Athens? Let me explain.

Paul had been run out of the last town he was speaking in and his friends made arrangements for him to go to Athens to wait for them as an attempt to keep him safe and out of harm's way. While waiting for his friends, he was out and about walking the city; tourist map in one hand and a digital camera in the other. (You get my drift!)

He was waiting for his friends to come and get him and in the process he was out finding coffee shops, wine bars and restaurants for lunch. He was eating Moussaka, Lamb Kliftiko and Stifado!

He was chatting with whoever he could engage. He was doing the tourist thing in Athens! Paul was taking the time to get out a bit and while he was there, found himself at Mars Hill engaging a group of philosophers about the "Unknown God!"[49]

Our Engagement with People is Vital

The more we disengage from the world around us, the more our passion for the lost is blunted. When we limit our exposure to people around us, our zeal to see people connect with eternity is dulled and our fervour to reach people is reduced; our voice to people becomes muted! We miss the experiences of common grace.

In a recent article by Marv Fox for the *Baptist Standard*[50] he was quoting George Barna of the Barna Institute[51] on the topic of "Mega-themes in the US." He mentions that one mega-theme in US Christianity today is that **Christians are becoming more ingrown and less outreach-oriented.** He says "Christians are becoming more spiritually isolated from non-Christians than was true a decade ago."[52] He goes on to say that "We've done a great job building Christian ghettos."[53]

---

[49] Acts 17:23

[50] http://www.baptiststandard.com/index.php?option=com_myblog&show=Gravitational-pull.html&Itemid=114

[51] http://www.barna.org/

[52] http://www.baptiststandard.com/index.php?option=com_myblog&show=Gravitational-pull.html&Itemid=114

[53] http://www.baptiststandard.com/index.php?option=com_myblog&show=Gravitational-pull.html&Itemid=114

Plain View

When I was a missionary in Bangkok we were warned about creating "Christian Ghettos". Obviously the people we would feel the most comfortable around would be other missionaries; and that was the main problem. The only way we could truly learn the Thai language and customs of the country was to go out and mix with people. We went to markets, temples and shopping malls and practised our language; we bugged people asking them "What do you call this in Thai?" and "What do you call that?"

To really learn Thai we'd have to go to the food markets. My three year old son Daniel loved it! He'd touch the wriggling frogs and poke the live fish. My daughter hated it! Rebekah would walk around with her T-shirt up over her nose hating the smells, the looks and the prods from the locals. Denise and I felt like idiots sometimes asking the Thai names for this and that. But learn the language; we did!

What about you – do you touch the live fish or do you walk around with your T-Shirt over your nose?

As people desperate to communicate Christ to the people of Bangkok, we learned the language of Thailand. We had to go where people were and seek conversation with them. We went out of our way to interact with people so we could learn to speak the heart language of a nation. We practiced the culture, we connected with the culture and we learned first-hand what people were thinking and feeling.

We felt we needed to learn what a connection looked like and felt like before we could speak of Jesus to a nation saturated with a folk Buddhism and its multiplied strains of animistic beliefs in the supernatural. We had to learn the language as a way into the hearts of individuals and the wider community.

As cross-cultural communicators we found many triggers and touch points for Thai society. We used them to communicate Jesus and actually connect personally. We used folk stories, history and even some food experiences to communicate spiritual truth. We took certain words from the Thai language that spoke volumes in the Thai mind and sought to re-interpret them to communicate godly truth. We became very creative in the way we communicated the good news about Jesus and saw a lot of fruit from the exercise.

People Watching Vs. Authentic Connections
I've always loved people watching. I sit in cafes, train stations and airports and just look.

But you know we'll need to do more than "just look".

Connecting with people requires something more from us. We need to get out more and actually talk with people around us. Connection is a very subjective term; it's even a bit existential.

Connecting with people is vital if we are going to share with them our faith in Jesus Christ. I'll go as far to say it is impossible to speak to people about Jesus without a connection of some sort. Jesus had this ability to connect, whether it was with a crowd or with an individual.

People need to connect with us on a certain level before they will allow us to speak to them; they want to know us and develop a certain level of trust with us. We are no longer allowed the luxury of shouting out God's truth like the prophets of old – today we must earn the trust of others to speak about a Christ hiding in plain view.

I admit that communication in a 21st century context is elaborate, if we seek to truly touch our world we will need to understand the world we live in so we can speak to it. Some communicators can't be bothered to learn or to connect with today. I met a few missionaries like that too - they couldn't be bothered to learn the language and relied on translators for YEARS! After a while the Thais would grow bored with these people and no matter how good they were, they were usually ignored.

Plain View

When Paul spoke to the gathered crowd on Mars Hill in **Acts 17** he had their attention – they loved him. He had a discovered a touch point for the people there in the form of this "Unknown God." Nobody interjected until.... he spoke about the resurrection of Christ; always a tough truth to navigate.

If Paul were alive today and was preaching he could have maybe appealed to movies like *The Matrix* when Neo was brought back to life after being shot, or to Gandalf in *Lord of the Rings* when he returned to life no longer grey but now Gandalf the White. Maybe... as in Batman VS Superman we wonder is Superman really dead? LOL.

These are the secular prophets of our day when it comes to explaining the resurrection. There are many more illustrations of resurrection in popular culture we could use to make the connection. The concept of resurrection is a far more accessible theme in the 21st than it was in the first century thanks to modern media and films.

Here's the point though; common grace encourages us to look a little closer at our culture and see where God Himself has gone before to prepare the way. We need to LOOK and seek to find our Lord standing in plain view waiting to be discovered!

If we can see Him, we have an unmissable opportunity to join the conversations around us and speak about eternal and changeless truth. We get to identify those secular prophets who in turn become the trigger point for a conversation with our generation about spiritual truth.

Is this scary to anybody reading this? I'm concerned and I'm the author here! But here's the point, we need to learn that we are operating in a Christian knowledge vacuum; the knowledge of God via scripture, tradition and experience is non-existent with many of the people we speak to today. They have no knowledge.... yet remain hardwired to receive truth. We need to become like missionaries or cross-cultural communicators to the world around us and discover the touch points and the triggers that initiate conversation.

How does it work?
Well, I was having my hair cut recently and was chatting away with Rob, my hairdresser, when a song familiar to me came on the sound system. I knew it was his iPod playing his music and so casually said "Oh Rizzle Kicks! Down with the Trumpets."

He looked at me stunned! "You know this song?" "Yeah sure, we play it pre and post service in our church." He was totally blown away and we started talking about our church. Moments later the next song happened to be by Example – which I also recognised and told him I have used this song to introduce my message last Sunday night.

The lyric goes like this; "If we don't kill ourselves, we'll be the leaders of a messed up generation." I told him how I had used the lyric to explain how I did see a lot of mess in this generation but also felt this generation above all others had potential to do extraordinary things. He was certainly amazed.

Now I know it was only a haircut! He hasn't come to church yet. He didn't fall down in the salon with repentance saying the Sinner's Prayer crying out "Jesus is Lord!" But... it was an opportunity to join a conversation and establish a "connection".

Comments from Rizzle Kicks and Example helped pave the way; they were the secular prophets that day. I'd like to think that maybe the next time a Christian speaks to him he might be a little closer to accepting Jesus.

Some people ask me why I play popular songs in our foyer from the radio in our pre-service and post- service. To me it's a no brainer: **It is a big ask for many people today to come to Church.** They rock up to this warehouse full of very welcoming and passionate people and they sort of freak out a bit - until they hear a song they recognise

Plain View

playing through the sound system. It's a familiar sound; hopefully they relax just a bit. (For those asking - we do vet the play list to make sure there are no songs blatantly promoting, sex and drugs. I make sure there is no swearing in the lyrics as well!)

Secular Prophets

I loved *The Matrix* trilogy! (I know it's old now – 2003!) But how does it all work? Well, one of the characters in the film is the Oracle. She's played by Gloria Foster in the first two movies. She is a mysterious cigarette smoking, cookie baking grandma that has the power of foresight which she uses to help Neo fight the ubiquitous Matrix! I found her character rather interesting. She's not what we as Christians may have chosen for an Oracle but she ends up being a perfect candidate for common grace.

What I love about the doctrine of common grace is that we don't get to choose who God ends up using to communicate His eternal power and divine nature; He chooses who He wants and just speaks!

Our joy is to discover these secular prophets in everyday life, in music and in film, on TV and on the news and give them voice. Jesus Christ is actually standing in plain view daring us to find Him and give Him voice! He's saying "Hello, it's me!"

There's a verse in 1 Peter that speaks about oracles. An oracle is like a prophet, a seer or sage. In my experience, there is nothing more potent to prepare people for change than a fresh account of the scripture. The King James Version says in **1 Peter 4:11** that "... if any man speak, let him speak as *the oracles of God*." Common grace requires us to not only take a closer look at modern culture but to be prepared and to be seeking the Holy Spirit for His help too.

Hang on here... first you say "take a closer look" then you say we need the help of the Holy Spirit; yeah! What's your problem? We do all we can do so the Holy Spirit is free to do what ONLY the Holy Spirit can do.

It's common grace that leads people to the doorstep of special grace.

Jesus has embedded Himself into many aspects of popular culture, He is standing in plain view and we need the help of the Holy Spirit to see Him there and also find the courage to speak about Him.

The Holy Spirit's main task is to reveal Jesus[54] – let's work with the Holy Spirit in this important undertaking.

We remain convinced of, as well as committed to, the fact that the Bible is the source document that reveals Jesus Christ, and people will never see Jesus if we don't tell them what the Bible says. We need the Holy Spirit's help to speak as oracles.

Thankfully there is no one more committed to bringing revelation and transformation into a person's life than the person of the Holy Spirit. Seek His enabling that you might speak "as the oracles of God."[55]

Heroes
Our culture today appears to be quite fascinated by heroes; not just the now defunct TV series but more those people we regard as persons of bravery, courage or just sheer guts! Have we considered why? What is it about heroes that trip the hardwiring inside of each of us? From Katniss Everdeen to Luke, from Kung Fu Panda to maybe the guy in Deadpool, heroes are important. The cult of celebrity is powerful from Justin to Bruno, from Taylor to Elli – people are fascinated by celebrity.

While mingling in the foyer of church the other Sunday, I asked a group of children which super hero was their favourite, Batman, Superman or Spiderman. The 3 years old boy looked me square in

---

[54] John 16: 12 - 15
[55] 1 Peter 4:11

Plain View

the face and with passion said, "Gok Wan![56]" I asked the mother, who was quite clearly amused, what her child was watching on TV; it is *so* time for him to go to school. NOW!

So what is it about heroes? It seems there is a pantheon of heroes, superstars and celebrities that garner the worship, attention and adoration of this generation. We have heroes for every day, every taste and for every mutant super power. Sort of like the pantheon of gods from the first century and with some of them we find the credentials of a secular prophet or oracle.

An uncompromising Christ stands in plain view eager to engage our hearts and minds

A number of years ago our church took the TV series *Heroes* and used it as a vehicle of common grace. It was fun! It was like going to Church but with popcorn!

We took some time (about 5 minutes out of 35 minutes) to explore the various characters and played clips from the show hoping to establish a bit of a connection with the 21st century audience.

We used the principles of common grace to lead us to special grace and opened up a conversation with people who weren't yet connected with Christ. It was a risky series but it was worth it as so many people came to faith in Jesus Christ.

Would anyone today dare to regard Jesus as a hero? Few would say yes, in the classical sense of a hero. But can anyone see Jesus Christ as brave, daring or "a man of steel"? Maybe some; and I am not taking anything away from his humanity.

I propose that we just can't afford to dismiss this rich texture of paint upon a society's canvas any longer. We simply can't hide behind a 20th century Church, a Church that became increasingly ignored. Like

---

[56] http://www.channel4.com/programmes/how-to-look-good-naked

Paul in Athens, we can venture out onto the stage of gods and goddesses and see if we can't find something out there to use to get people thinking about an unknown God.

I believe we are in a moment of time where the inherent spirituality of people is being "tripped". All over the world people are beginning to search for eternal truth. People's innate spirituality is being stimulated and they are embarking on a personal journey; searching for truth. I believe it is a most important and momentous time, unparalleled in all of human history where we are verging on a global awakening of unmatched force. God is at work here preparing this planet for a massive revealing of His Son who has come to rescue the world.

With eternity in their hearts, we stand in a time and an era unequal to anything we have ever seen and we are entering a time on Earth which will become the most extensive search for God ever recorded. By dissecting this global thirst for the supernatural, this hunger for the mysteries of life, the Church is forcefully advancing - prepared with a message about an irresistible Jesus and a journey of such great importance.

As Craig Detweiler expressed in his book *A Matrix of Meaning*, "We believe a bold, ancient, radical Christ stands on the side-lines of the culture wars, waiting with arms wide open, eager to engage our hearts, our minds and our culture!" [57]

In every way, Jesus is greater than any super hero you could ever imagine. He is wild, untamed and fierce. He is at times frightening in His power, alarming in His nature and positively fearsome when unleashed! Yet, His love is stronger! His love is the strongest love you will ever experience in your life.

---

[57] Craig Detweiler and Barry Taylor, (2003),*A Matrix of Meanings: Finding God in Pop Culture*, Baker Academic

Plain View

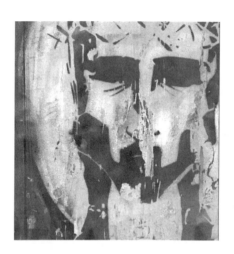

Part Two – Re-presenting Jesus Christ to a Waiting World

Plain View

Buddha never claimed to be God. Moses never claimed to be Jehovah. Mohammed never claimed to be Allah. Yet Jesus Christ claimed to be the true and living God. **Anonymous**

England has two books; the Bible and Shakespeare. England made Shakespeare, but the Bible made England. **Victor Hugo, (1802-1885) French writer.**

Jesus is God spelling Himself out in language that men can understand. **S.D. Gordon**

Every coin has two sides. **Anonymous**

Chapter 4: The Deity of Christ

Renaissance artists have used the subject matter surrounding Christ's deity in many ways; from da Vince to Raphael, from Botticelli to Fra Angelico; the deity of Christ has always held a certain primacy to these artists.

This truth, the deity of Jesus Christ, is what is referred to by Christian scholars as "dogma;" theology that is irrefutable and truth foundational to Christian belief. Jesus Christ is God; is equal with God and is by very nature God.[58]

FF Bruce & WJ Martin say this about the deity of Christ: "The belief in the deity of Christ is derived directly from statements concerning Him in the Bible. The references are so many and their meaning so plain, that Christians of every shade of opinion has always regarded its affirmation as ***an absolute and indispensable*** requisite of their faith."[59]

---

[58] Philippians 2:6: "Who, being in very nature God, did not consider equality with God something to be grasped."

[59] F.F. Bruce & W.J. Martin, *The Deity of Christ*. Manchester: North of England Evangelical Trust,
1964. Pbk. pp.24.

There are a number of great books about systematic theology so I won't repeat the information here. I will though seek to emphasise some aspects of Christ's deity we may have ignored, forgotten and may not have closely considered.

Vital to Our Ecclesiology[60] and Missiology[61]

The subject of the deity of Jesus Christ is not just an academic issue, concentrating upon the scholarly proof texts etc. The subject is practical, concrete and vital to our ecclesiology and missiology. Possessing a sound and workable, I repeat *"workable,"* understanding of the deity of Christ is absolute and indispensable; it's essential to our 21st century context.

The deity of Christ is an objective truth and we are called to communicate it as a subjective reality. If Jesus Christ is not the Son of God, equal with the Father, then Christianity's special significance in the world simply disintegrates. Our beliefs become as normal (or bizarre) as any others in the great pantheon of spiritual beliefs. If we can't communicate this great truth, our gospel is without power and authority.

If Jesus Christ is not the unique Son of God, equal with the Father, then His work at Calvary loses its redemptive significance and our mission is simply left in tatters. But we need to practice the significance of this truth in our church, in our preaching and witness if our mission is to be authentic in a 21st century pre-Christian world. It's not just a piece of theology or a combination of proof texts.

This high and holy doctrine must also become as real and as pragmatic to us as practitioners for it to work in every culture, in every nation and be translated into every tongue. This hallowed and divine truth must be able to be dragged through the mud and grime of real world scenarios and still perform.

---

[60] Doctrine of the Church

[61] Doctrine of our mission to proclaim Christ to the world

As elevated and sky-scraping as this doctrine is in all of Christendom, it must be able to get ***down and dirty*** and actually work in this hostile and brutal environment we call planet Earth. Our mission relies upon us being able to translate the truth of scripture into an everyday experience. What we need is the ability to drag this truth into the dirt and dust of a messy humanity and take into places polite people don't go. If it doesn't, then this truth remains as unapproachable as many regard Christ today; untouchable, defunct, invalid, non-operational, impotent and simply redundant!

Jesus Redefines God
Classic theology taught in a class room begins with "Theology Proper: The Theology of God." At least that's how they taught it at the Bible College I went to[62]. It's great for a class room experience and a book outline but the New Testament gives us a very different perspective and a powerfully different approach.

The New Testament totally and fundamentally redefines and redevelops who God is based upon who Jesus is. In fact, it is now impossible to understand or even know God unless you first connect with Jesus. All roads do not lead to God. You cannot even know the God of the Old Testament unless you first know the Jesus Christ of the New Testament.

You must first believe on the Lord Jesus Christ, call upon His name and change your mind about Him. There is no other road, no other avenue and no other way to know the God of the Old Testament unless you first know Jesus.

It becomes our job and our mission to make this unpalatable truth, as some would see it, both tasty and appealing; you know... bring out

---

[62] Commonwealth Bible College – 1976 – 1978 (Now called Alphacrucis – The Australian Christian Church's (formerly known as Assemblies of God in Australia-AOG) formal training institute - http://alphacrucis.edu.au/about/our-history/

the God flavours in the world. Like the incarnation of Jesus, it is our mission to make flesh of this truth.

Pretty high calling, hey?

Jesus made the point really clear in **John 14:6:** "I am the way and the truth and the life. *No one comes to the Father except through me."* Not a way but the way!

Peter was correct in **Acts 4:12** when he said "Salvation is found in *no-one else*, for there is *no other name* under heaven given to men by which we must be saved."

And again in **1 Peter 3:18** when he wrote, "For Christ died for sins once for all, the righteous for the unrighteous, *to bring you to God."*

After the death and resurrection of Jesus, no one could know God any other way, except through Him. In our modern class room, we may probably need to restart our Biblical training by first learning the theology of Christ. As we read the New Testament we understand that Jesus has deeply and fundamentally changed everything. Jesus had become the new definition of God.

Jesus was God
Throughout the gospel accounts, Jesus repeatedly stated He was God. The religious leaders of His day were not outraged because He was simply a good man or that He did miracles (although some of His actions did disturb them), they were outraged by the repeated declaration that Jesus made concerning His divinity, His origins and His authority.

In the writings of Mark we understand the religious rulers condemned Jesus to death based upon His assertions that He was God. In their eyes it was blasphemy. Mark's account read this way: "Again the high priest asked him, "Are you the Christ, the Son of the Blessed One?" "I am," said Jesus. "And you will see the Son of Man sitting at the right hand of the Mighty One and coming on the clouds of heaven." The high priest tore his clothes. "Why do we need any more witnesses?" he asked. "You have heard the blasphemy. What do you think?" They all condemned him as worthy of death." **Mark 14:61-64**

Claiming to be God was not an everyday claim made by ordinary people. Jesus claimed He was God and that He was the Son of God. No one was forcing Jesus to make this claim; Jesus Himself makes the claim that He was God.

My overriding desire is that you can capture a clearer, more perfect vision of the godhood of Jesus for the 21st century and seek to not just embrace His deity for yourself afresh but to communicate this truth with power.

One of my main goals is to address the disparity or inconsistencies of modern perceptions concerning Jesus and to challenge a "reboot of our ministry systems" to accommodate the power of this truth.

This is a foundational premise; our theology of Christ will profoundly affect our theology of the Church and our understanding of our mission in the world. How we view Christ and what we really believe about Him will affect the way we communicate Him. Put simply, our Christology affects our Ecclesiology and our Missiology – and maybe not too "simply"... but more profoundly!

With a clear New Testament picture of Jesus, it becomes the Church's desire to connect people with the Jesus of eternity so that the perceptions and pictures they hold about Jesus are in line with scripture and the facts portrayed in the Bible.
When Jesus said, "If you have seen me you have seen the Father"[63], it changed everything. Of course we know Jesus did change everything. He inaugurated a new agreement between us and God.

---

[63] John 14:9

He brokered a new covenant. **Hebrews 8:6** says "But the ministry Jesus has received is as superior to theirs as the covenant of which he is mediator is superior to the old one, and it is founded on better promises."

Jesus has forever altered our understanding of God.

Frost & Hirsch in their book *Re-Jesus*[64] put it this way: "It is clear from the New Testament that Jesus fundamentally alters the way we understand everything about God and faith. He affects every aspect of Christian doctrine and gives distinction to its understanding of God, humanity, sin, salvation and the eschaton (end times)."

Listen to their words; "He [Jesus] affects every aspect of Christian doctrine!"

God can now only be understood through Jesus. Jesus is now, according to **Colossians 2:9-10,** the one in whom, "... all the fullness of the Deity lives in bodily form... who is the Head over every power and authority." As those who may have had a classic theological education, we may need some time to rethink our beliefs and how they relate to scripture and the 21st century.

The Devil has a clear strategy for many Churches. He wants you to talk about God but not to say too much about Jesus Christ. God is easy to navigate – it's a small word with loads of meaning to the listener.

The central personage of Christianity though is Christ; who was God. John put it this way at the beginning of his gospel **John 1:1,** "In the beginning was the Word, and the Word was with God, and the Word was God."

---

[64] *ReJesus: A wild Messiah for a Missional Church*, Hendrickson Publishers & Stand Publishers, page 130

Re-presenting or Representing

How do we then re-present Jesus to the 21st century with all of His power, mystery and passion? How do we explain to a scientific and an online world the supernatural nature of Jesus? How do we explain a Jesus of miracles, of signs and wonders?

How do we re-present to a world on a spiritual journey when they have no image of Jesus? How do we describe the transforming power of a relationship with Jesus when the world today has turned their back on Him while others just simply have no knowledge of Him?

This dilemma is a common one for foreign missionaries. When we moved to Thailand to begin our missionary experience, we were faced with a similar situation: We were faced with a people who for thousands of years had been influenced by Buddhism and Hinduism as well as countless folk religions.

The Thai people were an incredibly "spiritual" people but had no knowledge of Jesus Christ. In their own language the name for God – Phra Jaew – is also the name for their king. Explaining the meaning from a Christian theology was difficult and fraught with so many problems.

In Indonesia, the name of God is Allah – this name is used in Christian worship to mean the God of the Bible – yet in Malaysian churches it is outlawed and kept to refer only to the Muslim God who is called Allah. Again, many problems exist.

In the days of Paul as he was on his journeys around Asia Minor and Europe, he was also confronted with a plethora of Gods. Diana, Cybele and Artemis, just to name a few, were highly revered. Ubiquitous to the day was the overriding worship of a *man* regarded as God and this was Caesar.

Not trying to be too simplistic, because communicating in the 21st century is highly complicated and intricate, but our only mission is to

"... know Jesus Christ and Him crucified." We are compelled to communicate Him ".... not with wise and persuasive words, but with a demonstration of the Spirit's power, so that [people's] faith might not rest on men's wisdom, but on God's power."[65]

We have come to believe that people are on a spiritual journey of discovery — we are called alongside them to nudge them in the direction of Jesus Christ. We do this with stories and "parables" — things that people can grasp that contain nuggets of spiritual truth that will reveal Jesus.

Jesus said in **Matthew 3:11**, "You've been given insight into God's kingdom. You know how it works. Not everybody has this gift, this insight; it hasn't been given to them. Whenever someone has a ready heart for this, the insights and understandings flow freely. But if there is no readiness, any trace of receptivity soon disappears. That's why I tell stories: to create readiness, to **nudge** the people toward receptive insight."

I love the Message translation of this scripture; look at how he says it. "You have been given insight..." It's Holy Spirit insight to communicate Jesus who is God. It's supernatural insight into people to determine how ready their hearts are. It's insight to tell a story or give an example that nudges people towards a ready and, ultimately, a receptive heart so they will believe in Jesus who is God.

"This is why I tell stories: to create readiness and to nudge people towards receptive insight."[66] We work in tandem with culture, the Holy Spirit and our own ability to be creative! Our goal is to present Jesus as God; eternal, immortal and powerful. Behold the miracle of common grace!

---

[65] 1 Corinthians 2:4-5
[66] Matthew 13:13-23

Take care of just introducing people to God. It sounds less threatening and less intellectually encroaching but in the end it is fruitless. People can only know God through Jesus Christ who is God.

Our desire and express mission is to lift up a true, authentic and accessible Jesus who is truly classic. The mission is clear; to communicate a Jesus who is not just retro but unforgettable in His reality and desire to know you personally.

We need to speak about and live out our story about a Jesus who is utterly fascinated by people, who loves all kinds of people and possesses the eternal power necessary to bring salvation and transformation. A Jesus so supernatural He can do all that He wishes to share and dispense kindness, compassion and love towards anyone – a Jesus rich in grace, abounding in mercy and abundant with favour towards you.

This is Jesus! And He is ancient, timeless, eternal and utterly in love with people so diverse and different. He is interested in every facet of who you are, you daily life, your trials and tribulations, your joys and your discoveries, your loves and your hurts – a Jesus fascinated with who you are, your destiny and future!

G.K. Chesterton[67] once said "The Christian ideal has not been tried and found wanting; it has been found difficult and left untried."[68]

The Name of Jesus
Many will ask; "Who is this man?" Let's start with His name – Jesus Christ. It carries deep significance and meaning; it simply means the vehicle of God's salvation. His name has power and it has authority; not like a magical incantation but as we speak His name we communicate His living and eternal power.

---

[67] English writer and Christian apologist (1874 -1936)
[68] Chapter 5, *What's Wrong With The World*, 1910

Jesus means God's salvation; Christ means anointed One and is the Greek rendering of the word "Messiah" which carries not only an idea, but a promise of salvation so extensive, so supernatural as to have spawned hope and an expectation among Jews for generations.

His name describes not only His mission but His nature; that He steps in from eternity to walk the roads of Israel to show us what God is like. Out of the timelessness of Heaven – begotten not created – ruler of the universe mysteriously connected with His Father and the Holy Spirit – creator of the heavens and the Earth – creator of man and woman. He reveals Himself as God – He is Deity – He is Divine. There is none like Him.

His divinity is essential to our understanding of Him. His divinity never violates, does damage to or infringes on the divinity of God; but Jesus Christ recalibrates, develops and furthers the revelation of who God is. Every one of the earliest followers of Christ came to a powerful resolve that they were called to worship Jesus.

The early Church was not birthed with a theology or debates about God; the Church had Jesus as their vision and centre of attention. Jesus begins with this concept in **John 10:9**, "I am the gate; whoever enters through me will be saved."

He continues with these thoughts further in **John 10:27-30**; "My sheep listen to my voice; I know them, and they follow me. I give them eternal life, and they shall never perish; no-one can snatch them out of my hand. My Father, who has given them to me, is greater than all; no-one can snatch them out of my Father's hand. I and the Father are one."

You can see why the religious rulers wanted to kill Him! First He says He is the gate – not Temple worship, not the obedience to the law and not sacrifices. He is the gate and whoever enters through Him will be saved. He then follows through with the metaphor explaining that He gives eternal life. Clearly, He was also saying that He is the entry point for the knowledge of God. He finishes up with the thought that He and the Father are one.

The early Church was fascinated with Jesus; and rightly so. They understood that it was Jesus who had explained who God was – Jesus was revealing God's nature. They knew that Jesus was the one who "made Him known."[69] It was for this reason they were able to rescue Christianity from becoming a back water Jewish cult and have it launched upon a waiting world with power.

If we are committed to lifting up Jesus, then we too will see this explosive movement of people towards Him, from hipster churches like Hillsong New York to radical youth filled churches like ours. But here is our point, we need the supernatural ability of the Holy Spirit to connect people with Him. We also need new strategies, new touch points and innovative ways to trip the internal hardwiring of a generation to literally see Him in all of His glory.

The writer to the Hebrews dispels all doubt in his poetic and potent depiction of Christ in **Hebrews 1:1-3**: "In the past God spoke to our forefathers through the prophets at many times and in various ways, *but in these last days he has spoken to us by his Son*, whom he appointed heir of all things, and through whom he made the universe. The Son is the radiance of God's glory and the exact representation of his being, sustaining all things by his powerful word. After he had provided purification for sins, he sat down at the right hand of the Majesty in heaven." [Emphasis added]

We can only know God through Jesus Christ. So we must know Him to declare Him to the entire world. Jesus changed the meaning of the word "God" – He has altered our understanding of God. We now know God through Jesus Christ. Jesus reframed our knowledge of God.

---

[69] John1:18

Christianity is not a follow on from Judaism. Christianity was never meant to be a Jewish sect or cult. Even though Jesus was Jewish, He came to prove the Jewish texts and prophecies. Jesus has set us apart from Judaism and every other religion known or concocted by mankind since the beginning of time.

We cannot assume, presume or figure out Jesus Christ from what we think we know about the God of Israel! It's the other way around; we now get to know the God of Israel because we are related to and connected to Jesus. No man comes to the Father unless they come through Jesus Christ. No one – no not one person can know salvation unless they come through Jesus Christ the Son of God.

In these last days, God is speaking to us through His Son - He is the One. (Sorry Neo!)

Unleashed upon the Earth
Jesus desires His deity to be unleashed upon the world; His authority to touch every life, His miracle nature and eternal power to be let loose. His desire is for His character to capture our faith, our loyalty and our allegiance.

To be impacted by Jesus Christ requires us to be connected to deity; power beyond comprehension. This influence is supernatural and indeed the most powerful force in the entire universe. It is the power of the "... same spirit that raised Christ from the dead"[70]; it is salvation.

Our Christian adherence of faith revolves around this point; Jesus is Lord. There is salvation in no other name than the name of Jesus. The influence of the 21st century Church will be in its creative and original ways of telling and re-telling the old, old story.

---

[70] Romans 8:11

The impact of the 21st century Church at home in a hostile environment will be her ability to unswervingly communicate Jesus Christ and His death and resurrection using every bit of technology, employing every nuance and fine distinction our times avail us of.

The effectiveness of the 21st century Church will be measured by how well she declares the absolute divinity and potency of Jesus Christ as King of Kings, Lord of Lord, Alpha and Omega and the Beginning and the End.

Paul's words were written in a first century that looks so much like ours that it reminds us it all depends upon attitude; our approach to today, our outlook on society and our posture towards the people of our age. It is my firmly held belief that we sit on the verge of a powerful movement of people into the Church connecting with Jesus Christ. This can only be described as revival - it reminds me that what once took place in the first century can happen again in the 21st century - hundreds of thousands coming to Jesus and our churches bursting with people.

Please read the scripture that follows....

"Your attitude should be the same as that of Christ Jesus: Who, being in very nature God, did not consider equality with God something to be grasped, but made Himself nothing, taking the very nature of a servant, being made in human likeness. And being found in appearance as a man, he humbled himself and became obedient to death - even death on a cross! Therefore God exalted him to the highest place and gave him the name that is above every name, that at the name of Jesus every knee should bow, in heaven and on earth and under the earth, and every tongue confess that Jesus Christ is Lord, to the glory of God the Father." **Philippians 2:5-11**

Can we come down from the high and lofty perches of the prophets of old who thunder forth God's commands and take upon ourselves the very nature of servants; to offer an invitation to know the Lord of life?

Can we stop judging those outside the Church[71]; somehow expecting people to live like saints when in fact they are deep in offence, mired by the stench and stain of sin? Is it not possible for us, by the power of the Spirit, to demonstrate a love so strong that the dust of humanity and the sweat of its desperation can be overcome? Can we not approach this generation with a little bit of sweat and a bit of dust on our own faces as we live the power of the gospel in the world around us?

Can we present to this dying world a Saviour so supernatural, so miraculous and so outstanding that they will run into His open arms? Is it possible to lift up a Christ who can perform the miracle, heal the disease, bring wholeness to the broken heart and provide comfort to the abused and bashed down?

May we humble ourselves to be found in appearance as humans being as fellow journeymen in this harsh and hostile world so fallen and broken and go to others knowing that he is with us always "... even until the end of the earth; Amen."

Jesus is God; of this there is no doubt!

Alexander, Caesar, Charlemagne, and myself founded empires; but what foundation did we rest the creations of our genius? Upon force. Jesus Christ founded an empire upon love; and at this hour millions of men would die for Him. **Napoleon Bonaparte**
I never thought about Buddha becoming any real part [of my life] . . . Jesus is the only one I've ever been interested in. **Jack Kerouac, novelist and voice of the "Beat Generation".**

---

[71] 1 Corinthians 5:12

There is an angel inside of this rock and I am setting him free. **Michelangelo on the block of granite that became the statue of David.**

I'm a Muslim, but I think Jesus would have a drink with me. He would be cool. He would talk to me. **Mike Tyson.**

Chapter 5: The Humanity of Jesus

The early work of El Greco (1541 – 1614), reveals how popular the theme of the humanity of Christ was to its day. His magnificent painting of the *Healing of the Blind Man* is a renaissance glimpse of His human side.

Jesus was born of The Virgin and experienced thirty years of normal out-of-the-limelight life followed by three years of public ministry. These days of obscurity revealed His humanity in dusty profiles. As we explore it further, we discover it was an outrageous plan packed with scandal... and God was the perpetrator.

The incarnation was an idea conceived before the foundations of the world, in the eternal and infinite mind of God. It was a plan so well guarded that we in this century are still considering its reach. "He [God] destroyed the wisdom of the wise and frustrated the intelligence of the intelligent."[72]

The "en-fleshment" of Jesus was a mystery so shrouded and cloaked in intrigue that even the angels wondered at God's actions. It was a hidden wisdom and a plan no one could have possibly figured out on their own.
1 Corinthians 2:7-8 says, "No, we speak of ***God's secret wisdom***, a wisdom that has been ***hidden*** and that God destined for our glory before time began. None of the rulers of this age ***understood it,*** for if they had, they would not have crucified the Lord of glory." God said "I will come and become flesh and live amongst them."

---

[72] 1 Corinthians 1: 19

The Incarnation

The impossible made possible by the work of the Holy Spirit. The infinite fuses with the finite. The seed of God impregnates a virgin. Deity takes upon itself the flesh of humanity. How can this be? God's essence impregnates a virgin's womb, the result of this miracle then drawing upon the woman's nutrients and her very life. Could this work?

Jesus was born in a stable behind a hotel; He clothed Himself in human flesh, born human – yet still somehow possessed the divine nature of God even as a babe wrapped in swaddling clothes. Mystery! How could this work?

Son of God and Son of Man – "... but made himself nothing, taking the very nature of a servant, being made in human likeness."[73] A self-imposed restriction upon His divinity was His choice and plan. He became flesh.

He was God in flesh; and being found in appearance as a man, he humbled himself and through the outstanding miracle of the virgin birth Jesus steps on to the stage of Time & Space. He was limited by flesh yet still the possessor of deity. God yet still Man – "God of very God and man of very man." Unheard of in the annals of Heaven's and Human history the God/Man comes to Earth – a divine nature wrapped in a human nature; unbelievable – but true!

He was 100% human while maintaining the fact He was 100% divine. How could it be? Behold the wonder, the complexity and love of God; behold the extent the Divine is willing to go to so we as humans can be reunited with our God.

Paul's declaration is found in **Romans 1:3**: "... regarding his Son, who as to his human nature was a descendant of David."

---

[73] Philippians 2:7

The Scandal of the Incarnation

His was a scandalous arrival. Most modern people living in the 21st century will relate to this kind of scandal! Jesus' mother was about 16 years of age, she had conceived before she was married and the message wasn't lost on her village either. Joseph did the right thing and married her to save her from any further shame. 9 months later she gave birth behind a hotel in a stable surrounded by farm animals. Scandal!

But here is the greatest scandal – not that Mary conceived out of wedlock but that she claimed it was God who appeared to her one night and she became pregnant by the Holy Spirit and that her child would be called the Son of God.

To further complicate this scandal, Joseph corroborated the story with one of his own. He claimed an angel of the Lord came and told him that the child within her womb was Christ, Messiah, and that he should take Mary as his wife.

You want to know the greatest of all scandal though; is that God decided to become human and take upon Himself flesh and blood; to live, breath and walk with sinful man on an Earth infected by sin and ruled by the Evil One[74].

"For in Christ all the fullness of the Deity lives in bodily form."
Colossians 2: 9

How could this be possible? Did the trinity suffer some violation? Did a schism appear in the trinity to allow for the en-fleshment of Jesus? What we know for a fact is that Christ, the Son of God, literally took upon Himself flesh and blood and agreed to live with us so we could see and understand God.

---

[74] 2 Corinthians 4:4

It was impossible for us to reach Heaven and so God conceived this strategy to come down and reach out to us. This is true scandal; that God who lives in unapproachable light, in unbearable holiness and in untouchable beauty took upon Himself the flesh and blood body of a child to be born in rude fashion behind a hotel in a stable populated by farm animals. He was to allow Himself to be handled, touched and changed as a baby; to suck at the breast of Mary His mother *like any other child born to mankind.* Mind blowing stuff right there!

So powerful was His humiliation – so scandalous His journey from the beauty of Heaven – so outrageous His incarnation – so shocking was His descent into humanity... yet He "did not abhor the virgin's womb" because this was a plan begotten in the mind of Deity from before the whole world was formed and created.

Will any of us ever be able to imagine the humiliation of the incarnation? Will anyone ever be able to plumb the depths of such love? How was it possible for God of very God to become Man of very Man? How was it possible for God in Deity to be expressed on Earth in full Humanity? And yet it happened – in the annals of history it now takes its unassailable pride of place. This very action of God split time and eternity.

For many around the world this is the focus of Christmas. But it was His humiliation; it was the scandal, it was the outrage, it was the utter and absolute divine embarrassment of the act; how could it be that God would reveal His love for mankind in such a powerful and yet wonderful way?

This is the reasons the angels sing! This is the reason the shepherds were glorifying God and singing! This is the reason the Men from the East arrived with such lavish gifts – this is the reason kings and governments quaked with fear.

God, who dwells in Heaven, is safe but what would happen when He had taken upon Himself flesh and blood and had come to live with mankind?! Jesus Christ was human; He had a human lineage. He had a body; He came in the flesh. He might have had His mother's eyes or His grandfather's nose! This is the incarnation. This is God coming to the world though Jesus Christ.

Jesus in His humanity was outstanding; He was sinless Himself, yet merciful to sinners; meek under provocation, yet with refined sensibility; dignified, yet without arrogance; pure, yet with a deep insight into evil; He was accessible to people and He never hid from those in need. He never misunderstood nor discouraged any sincere seeker.

Earthly princes look greatest at a distance, surrounded with pomp; but He needed no earthly state, for the more closely He is viewed, the more He stands forth in peerless majesty, sinless and divine. He rested His teaching on His own authority, and the claim was felt by all.

He was utterly void of resentment for wrongs, even wrongs against himself. When apprehended, instead of sharing the disciples' indignation, He rebuked them; instead of condemning His murderers He prayed for them: "Father, forgive them, for they know not what they do" (Luke 23:34). He was a champion to those who were downtrodden and embarrassed – to the woman caught in adultery, He was the supplier of grace and compassion, not his judgement and condemnation.

He was a Real Man
In the book *Vintage Jesus*[75], written by veteran wild man Mark Driscoll, he says; "Jesus was a dude." I love it. Driscoll seeks to tell us that Jesus was a real man. He uses colourful language to further describe Jesus as a man.

---

[75] Crossway USA (16 May 2008) – Page 31

He goes on to say, "Because Jesus worked in a day when there were no power tools, he likely had calluses on his hands and muscles on his frame and did not look like so many of the drag-queen Jesus images that portray him with long, flowing, feathered hair, perfect teeth, and soft skin, draped in a comfortable dress accessorized by matching open toed sandals and handbag."

As an author he takes his poetic license to the limit when he says, "Jesus did not have Elton John or the Spice Girls on his iPod, the View on his TiVo, or a lemon-yellow Volkswagen Beetle in the garage." (I love the way Driscoll portrays the humanity of Jesus – though I think the Spice Girls were cool!)

Slightly more conservative than Driscoll let me quote FF Bruce[76].... He says this in regards to the humanity of Jesus Christ; "If Godhead is to be revealed in the created order, it will be revealed most adequately in manhood, since man was created in the image of God. It is fitting, then, that our Lord Jesus Christ, the Divine Word who became flesh, should in His one person be both altogether God and altogether man—not something betwixt and between."

He continues in his description by saying, "The more, then, we emphasize our Lord's real Humanity, the more we do justice to His true nature, for it is in that real humanity - *in* it, and not merely *through* it that we see the Godhead shine."

The Stoic Myth
When I was in Bible College, one of my fellow third year students asked to speak to me. He took me aside to bring some correction and began to say that in his opinion I was too much of a joker and if I really wanted to succeed in the ministry I needed to be a bit more serious.

---

[76] F.F. Bruce, (1973), The Humanity of Jesus Christ, Journal of the Christian Brethren Research Fellowship, page 5

Plain View

He said my joking around and constant use of humour was not a good trait in a future pastor. I needed to be a bit more stoic; like him. He said, "You know the Bible never records that Jesus ever smiled!" I listened with great interest as I respected this guy and hey, I was only nineteen years old, what did I really know about the ministry yet?

So from the beginning of that day I walked around attending my lectures, morning tea, lunch and dinner. I was trying really hard not to see the funny side of life.

This stoicism lasted for 36 hours – much longer than I thought it would in hindsight – until I broke free from the imposed seriousness of an older student. I think I ran through the college with 36 hours' worth of laughing up my sleeve!

In Thailand, I remember that every picture of His Royal Highness the King of Thailand was one of Him without a smile. The reason for his stoicism was that he was not the intended King of Thailand, it was his older brother who ascended the throne before him but his brother was shot and killed in a palace tragedy which was later covered up as a scandal. As a consequence, he never smiled in public and did so in honour of his murdered brother.

I have wondered for a long time now why it's supposed to be wrong to think of Jesus smiling or laughing. I have tried for decades now to understand why people think that not only did Jesus have no sense of humour but that we His servants should be bereft of a sense of one too. For years now I have tried to work out why God's servants have mostly been so severe, bereted of a smile and a hearty laugh and why Church was sooooo serious.

I vividly remember an occasion when I was preaching for a church and after the morning service we went to the pastor's home for dinner. We were all gathered around the table to pray for the food and during the prayer my son Daniel, all of 12 months old, passed wind!

After the "amen" – I laughingly apologised for my son's noises – I referred to it as a fluff (which I thought was very polite because I knew of *many* other words for the sound). To my utter surprise the husband, father and pastor looked at me with a not too impressed face and said these words which I will never forget; "Tom, in our family we don't even have a word for that!" (I nearly died!)

Thinking that was funny, (sorry – but to get a laugh out of most guys any kind of noise like that would suffice) I was just about to laugh when to my horror I realised that the pastor was absolutely serious and not one of his family members at the table was even cracking a smile!

I'm not too sure about everyone reading this book but I find it hard to believe that Jesus who had brothers and sisters didn't play games with each other and laugh out loud. I think it is unnatural to think that Jesus spent 3 years with 12 young rough and tumble men and they never cracked jokes or sat around the fire at night and laugh until they cried.

Jesus was 100% human, with human emotions and human abilities to smile and laugh. Laughter is almost an uncontrollable facility within humans; we were built to see the humorous side of life and to not laugh would, I think, break something on the inside! In my head I see a clear case for mistaken piety!

People loved Jesus – they enjoyed His company – He got party invites all the time – common non-religious people found His company attractive. They loved hanging out with Jesus! I find it hard to imagine a Jesus who never smiled and never laughed out loud! I find it unthinkable that Jesus didn't have a sense of humour and didn't tell jokes!

He was a Man!

Plain View

Jesus was a man and He was a strong man; He was compassionate and caring. He was a real man, He hung out with real guys; all twelve of his disciples were real men!

Jesus was masculine, manly, tough, intelligent, fit, was not afraid of hard work, yet He was sensitive towards the needs of women, the weak and those who were sick. He was gentle towards women and children and provided an atmosphere that they found safe and comforting.

He was a true liberator of women and an affirmer of men – He loved children and sought to provide for them a safe environment and a future hope. He was authoritative yet people wanted to be near him and even touch him. Thousands gathered for days without food just to hear him speak. He continued to draw crowds where ever He went!

He was a miracle worker. The impossible was His territory. He restored sight to the blind, He cured the lame, He provided the sick with true health and He was willing to make those who were sick with leprosy, well, and for those who were paralysed, walk. He was not a magician, a charlatan or an imposter but a true worker of God inspired miracles. With Him around there is nothing that was impossible.

He was supernatural; He walked on water, turned water into wine, calmed a raging sea, spoke to wind, took a boy's lunch of two fish and five loaves of bread and fed the multitudes of gathered people... with food left over! He was supernatural.

He had authority over demons and even the Devil himself was frustrated in his attempt to distract Him from His mission. With authority He cast out demons and set people free from the oppression of the Devil. He was unafraid; He was bold, fearless and undaunted by the powers of evil spirits.

His teachings were delivered with authority. They were relevant and easy to grasp, His teachings were easy to apply to everyday life. They were truth which set people free. People understood what He was saying and enjoyed listening to Him. **Mark 1:27-28**, "The people were all so amazed that they asked each other, 'What is this? A new teaching and with authority! He even gives orders to evil spirits and they obey him.' News about him spread quickly over the whole region of Galilee."

He walked in confidence. He was authoritative, commanding and people would follow Him. Many dropped what they were doing to follow Him immediately. The people of the first century Church were people who were so powerfully impressed and influenced by Him that they were willing to die for Him rather than deny Him.

He was the supreme sacrifice of God for a sin soaked world. He was the Lamb of God who had come to take away the sins of the world – He came as Saviour and Redeemer. He came to bring salvation, transformation and renewal to all who would believe on Him. He was the light of the world, the bread of life, the good shepherd willing to lay down His life for all. He came as the living water and whosoever would drink from Him would never thirst again.

He came as the supreme sacrifice for sin. Though he himself was sinless, He took the sin of the entire world. In His death He bought God's satisfaction against sin and reconciled to God all who would dare to believe upon Him and follow Him.
He died for sin and rose again to new life so we could experience transforming love and to walk in His new life. He rose again from death to utterly defeat the powers of Satan and place victory into the hands of all who would use His name, so that at the name of Jesus demons shudder with fear and darkness trembles in contemplation of the judgement to come!

This is no namby pamby Jesus, thin, emaciated and effeminate Jesus. This was Jesus the Son of the Living God, who is Alpha and Omega, the beginning and the end, the First and the Last. He is Messiah, the Christ, the anointed one of God who died and rose again from death never to die again. He is God of very God yet man of very man.

He is a God/Man. He understands and sympathises with each of us in our weaknesses and was tempted in all ways like us, yet He Himself is not weak. He forgives our sins, which only God can do, yet He remains sinless and sympathetic to each of us. He is timeless yet invades our space and time with miracle working power.

He is eternal but knows of our every waking moment. He is omniscient knowing everything yet is conscious of our every hurt, our every need and our every personal thought. He is God. He is Divine, but also human.

He is the One who was, who is and who is to come. He is the same yesterday, today and forever. He will never change and never waver in His love and concern for us. He is a God of grace bestowing upon us all of His goodness rather than giving us what we deserve. He is a miracle working God, intervening into our reality; meeting our every need. He stands ready to bless, not curse; to help, not hinder; and to give, not take from any of us! He is divine and wonderfully human. He is Divine Deity and Humanity personified.

Most of all, He is alive! Yes, He died to secure our salvation but He rose again from the dead, overcoming the enemies of Death and Hell to be with us and be our God. He is alive to hear our every prayer and our every desperate thought. He is alive to heal our heart and take from us the pains of a bitter world. He is alive to forgive us of our every sin. He is alive to fill us with His power and He is alive to help us find victory in our own personal battles with the Devil and his legions from Hell. He is alive to inspire us with a destiny. He is alive to anoint us with power. He is the Christ, the Son of Man, and the Son of the living God who died but is now alive, and alive for ever more; never to die again!

He is alive and is now preparing a place for us; in "(His) Father's house are many mansions and He is working to prepare a place for (us)"[77]. He is alive forever more and He is planning His return to our world again; this time not as a suffering saviour but as King of Kings.

Jesus will return a second time (as promised in the Bible) to bring this world to its conclusion where there will be peace and grace abounding. He will come to wipe away all our tears and make it all new. He has promised He is coming back a second time. Jesus said in **Revelation 22:20**, "Yes, I am coming soon." [And we respond ...] Amen. Come, Lord Jesus."

We are not talking about a religion here, we are speaking of a life changing relationship with the God who created all we see in this great Universe. We speak of a living and vibrant relationship with a God who loves us and desires to do only good for us. We speak of a God who in Jesus Christ came to show grace, not judgement; favour, not condemnation!

This Jesus of Bethlehem was to become the Saviour of the very world He had created. To all who would believe, He would become the atoning sacrifice for their sins. This same Jesus who suffered the shame and disgrace of human flesh is now exalted above all. He is high and lifted up!

He who was born behind an inn in a stable was also the One taken by cruel men and crucified. He was tortured and tormented by a group of Roman guards who viciously whipped Him and savagely placed upon His holy brow a crown not of gold but of thorns.

This Jesus, born in a stable surrounded by animals, is the same Jesus who hung upon the crude and wooden cross who died for our sins; His last words to his father in Heaven were "Forgive them for they know not what they do!"

---

[77] John 14:2

This same Jesus, declared dead, was placed in a tomb for three days and on the third day was raised from death by the power of the Holy Spirit – the corruption of death could not lay a hold of His body; the power of death could not hold Him in the ground – He arose triumphant over death to give new life to all who would simply believe upon Him!

Timothy succinctly puts it this way in **1 Timothy 3:16**, "Beyond all question, the mystery of godliness is great: He appeared in a body, was vindicated by the Spirit, was seen by angels, was preached among the nations, was believed on in the world, and was taken up in glory."

May I conclude this chapter with the words of the prolific evangelical Christian author, editor, publisher and journalist James C. Hefley, who once wrote these words about Jesus?

"Here is a man who was born in an obscure village... He never wrote a book. He never held an office. He never owned a home. He never had a family. He never went to college. He never put His foot inside a big city. He never travelled more than two hundred miles from the place where He was born. He never did one of the things that usually accompany greatness. He had no credentials but Himself. He had nothing to do with this world except the naked power of His Divine manhood."

"While still a young man, the tide of popular opinion turned against Him. He was turned over to His enemies. He went through the mockery of a trial. He was nailed to a cross between two thieves. His executioners gambled for the only piece of property He had on Earth while He was dying; and that was His coat. When He was dead He was taken down and laid in a borrowed grave through the pity of a friend."

"Such was His human life—He rises from the dead. Nineteen wide centuries have come and gone and today He is the centrepiece of the human race and the leader of the column of progress."

He concludes with these words, "I am within the mark when I say that all the armies that ever marched, and all the navies that ever were built, and all the parliaments that ever sat, and all the kings that ever reigned, put together, have not affected the life of man upon this Earth as powerfully as has that One Solitary Life."

This Jesus is irresistible – radical beyond all measure!

It was this same Jesus, the Christ who, among many other remarkable things, said and repeated something which, proceeding from any other being would have condemned him at once as either a bloated egotist or a dangerously unbalanced person. When He said He himself would rise again from the dead, the third day after He was crucified, He said something that only a fool would dare say, if he expected longer the devotion of any disciples—unless He was sure He was going to rise. No founder of any world religion known to men ever dared say a thing like that! **Wilbur Smith, bestselling author.**

The bodily resurrection of Jesus Christ from the dead is the crowning proof of Christianity. If the resurrection did not take place, then Christianity is a false religion. If it did take place, then Christ is God and the Christian faith is absolute truth. **Henry M. Morris, Christian apologist (1918 –2006).**

"Since the children have flesh and blood, he too shared in their humanity so that by his death he might break the power of him who holds the power of death—that is, the devil." **Hebrews 2: 14**

Chapter 6: The Death and Resurrection of Jesus Christ – a Dramatic Adaptation for the Big Screen

I find toilet graffiti interesting reading; purely from a philosophical point of view of course! I once read these words on a toilet door; "'God is dead.' Nietzsche." Right underneath was written "'Nietzsche is dead.' God."

I find it interesting what people say about Jesus Christ. For instance, **John Lennon** once said; "We're more popular than Jesus now; I don't know which will go first, rock 'n' roll or Christianity." Needless to say, the Beatles disbanded in 1970.

Sholem Asch, a Polish born Jew and prolific author, novelist and dramatist who wrote exclusively in Yiddish said these words about Jesus Christ; "Jesus Christ is to me the outstanding personality of all time, all history, both as Son of God and as Son of Man. Everything he ever said or did has value for us today and that is something you can say of no other man, dead or alive. There is no easy middle ground to stroll upon. You either accept Jesus or reject him."

C.S. Lewis, a leading figure at Oxford University, was an Irish novelist who was also famous as a scholar, academic and the creator of the popular children's books, "The Chronicles of Narnia". He said this about Jesus; "For a man who was merely a man and said the sort of things Jesus said would not be a great moral teacher. He would either be a lunatic or else he would be the Devil of Hell. You must make your choice. Either this man was, and is, the Son of God; or else a madman or something worse. You can shut Him up for a fool, you can spit at Him and kill him as a demon; or you can fall at His feet and call Him Lord and God. But let us not come with any patronizing nonsense about His being a great human teacher. He has not left that open to us. He did not intend to."

Whatever you think about Jesus there is one thing you cannot do and that is continue to ignore Him. His very life compels us, His actions oblige us and what He says about Himself requires us to come to some decision about Him. We cannot remain neutral.

It Is Finished!
Too many people think sympathetically and emotionally concerning the death of Jesus on the cross. Yes, it was painful and yes, Jesus did physically suffer and die. However, if you only see the emotional side you'll miss the eternal importance of what actually occurred on Calvary.

The Bible says Jesus was beaten, His flesh was torn and a crown of thorns was placed upon His head and He was then brutally crucified by a guard of Roman soldiers. The Bible actually says He was disfigured beyond human recognition[78].

---

[78] Isaiah 52:14

But His death was much more than a clean kill by the Roman Praetorian Guards or the tragic execution of a good man, even if you believe He was the Son of God.

The crucifixion was more a legal drama than divine performance. It was more judiciary than religious. It had more to do with the law and its righteous fulfilment than simply a good man condemned. If I could explain the crucifixion; it was more *Law & Order* than *CSI*, more John Grisham than Tom Clancy.

The crucifixion, inspired by a love unknown and unheard of to mankind, was in fact a legal arrangement between God and His Son and all of mankind were to benefit from it. It was a plan laid down from before the world was created hidden in the mind of Deity.[79] [80]

Jesus came to Earth as God's Son to live a life pleasing to His heavenly Father in every way. He became flesh through incarnation; He came to show us the glory of God. **John 1:14** says it this way; "The Word became flesh and made his dwelling among us. We have seen his glory, the glory of the One and only, who came from the Father, full of grace and truth."

He was brought to Earth to communicate to man who God was. **John 1:17-18** says "For the law was given through Moses; grace and truth came through Jesus Christ. No-one has ever seen God, but God the One and only, who is at the Father's side, has made him known." Mankind had, for a short period of time, a glimpse of the Father, in Christ.

His mission was to communicate to a world that had lost its connections with God and what God was like. He came as "the way the truth and the life."[81] He came to declare that anyone who

---

[79] 1 Peter 1:20
[80] 1 Corinthians 2:7
[81] John 14:6

believed on Him would have access to God the Father and enjoy relationship with the benefit of eternal life.

But here's the legal side to His incarnation; Jesus came as the perfect sacrifice for sins. Under the Old Testament laws, under the old agreements God had with mankind (and especially the nation of Israel), if anyone committed a sin they were required to bring a sacrifice for that sin to be atoned, or reconciled, with God. So when someone transgressed the law of God (sinned), a sacrifice was required and it was the blood of animals that covered their sin.

Jesus came into the world to be the ultimate and perfect sacrifice. This was the legal drama to be enacted before God the Father, the angels, the hosts of Hell, Satan, a Roman government, a religious government of Israel and on behalf of everyone who had ever lived and would ever live. Check out what the Bible says:

"God presented him as a sacrifice of atonement, through faith in his blood. He did this to demonstrate his justice." **Romans 3:25-26**

"This is love: not that we loved God, but that he loved us and sent his Son as an atoning sacrifice for our sins." **1 John 4:10**

"For Christ died for sins once for all, the righteous for the unrighteous, to bring you to God." **1 Peter 3:18**

"The death he died, he died to sin once for all; but the life he lives, he lives to God." **Romans 6:10**

His crucifixion was not just a bloody execution of simply a good man. This was no typical Roman execution. His brutal torture and death is not merely a scene we keep for Easter to weep over. This was to be the exercise of the justice of God upon a perfect and sinless sacrifice; Messiah had come. All of history had waited for this day. Jesus was arriving at the pinnacle of the judicial calendar to appease the anger of God against sinful man. He was the atoning sacrifice.

Plain View

Atonement is an act by which God restores a relationship of harmony and unity between Himself and human beings. He was to perform this through the death of His own Son. It would have eternal consequences.

Not only was Christ's death atonement, but it was also redemption. The concept of "redemption" is, again, a legal word; it means simply to be "bought back". Through the sacrifice of Jesus upon the cross, He was to become our Redeemer. The purchase price was His blood, we were to be bought back from sin's power over our lives, bought back from Satan's authority over our lives and bought back to be a people who can now worship God in an open, family relationship.

Listen to this: "Christ redeemed us from the curse of the law by becoming a curse for us, for it is written: 'Cursed is everyone who is hung on a tree.' He redeemed us in order that the blessing given to Abraham might come to the Gentiles through Christ Jesus, so that by faith we might receive the promise of the Spirit." **Galatians 3:13-14**

"For you know that it was not with perishable things such as silver or gold that you were redeemed from the empty way of life handed down to you from your forefathers, but with the precious blood of Christ, a lamb without blemish or defect." **1 Peter 1:18-19**

His last words were the culmination of His passion and His final declaration to all the powers and authorities. He knew why He was there. He knew it was the will of God for Him to suffer and die. It was a plan established.

The lead up to the cross and its pain and His suffering all the indignities he experienced in His body was nothing in comparison to the experience of literally becoming sin for us. Remember this; the Holy Son of God who knew no sin ***became sin*** for us. **2 Corinthians 5:21** says "God made him who had no sin to be sin for us, so that in him we might become the righteousness of God."

The horror of all this culminated on the cross of Calvary. It was not the beatings, it was not the torture, nor was it the mockery that was the greatest pain suffered by Jesus that day. Rather, it was that moment when He became sin for us; this was the moment when the unimaginable became a reality. Was the fabric of the Trinity somehow warped by the separation inevitably caused by the sin of the whole world imputed to Jesus? Heaven will tell the story.

It was a moment of cosmic impact as in utter amazement demons watched on with glee as the tormentor of their souls was crucified. It was a moment of complete and sheer unbelief as Lucifer, Star of the Morning watched in a confused daze as he witnessed the death of God's Son upon the cross of Calvary. "Was it that simple?" he thought.

The scripture says in **1 Corinthians 2:8** that "None of the rulers of this age understood it, for if they had, they would not have crucified the Lord of glory." Hell hadn't understood the divine plan. Satan was not privy to this secret proposal. All of Hell was not able to fathom the hidden wisdom of God's plot. Satan remained clueless as he watched the final moments of Jesus' life eek way.

But the reality would soon come crashing in on him and his dark, nefarious kingdom.

This justice of God upon His Son was about to throw the kingdom of darkness into such total chaos and absolute disarray. If only Satan had known; had the domain of darkness only known, they would not have colluded to crucify Jesus the Son of God! Had Satan understood the coming consequences, he would not have stirred the crowd to shout out "Crucify Him – give us Barabbas!"

Meanwhile back on Calvary's mount on Golgotha, the place of the Skull, Jesus was suspended between Earth and Heaven brutally nailed to a wooden cross. It was there, the perfect unity of God in Trinity came under enormous and unimaginable pressure. Was the

Plain View

fabric of the universe about to be torn and ruptured or would His death inaugurate and new and living way?[82]

Jesus is heard crying out in more pain than He had ever known in all of eternity. It was a searing pain such that Deity had never experienced; it was the moment when sin came upon the One who had known no sin. Holiness transcended by the utter horror of man's abject iniquity!

There was a deafening stillness when the heavens watched on in terror as their champion and beloved Lord was marred by the blunt force trauma of the power of sin. Angels were seen in noiseless repose shocked by the utter horror, they lined the balconies of Heaven silently weeping unable to even look at each other as they witnessed the dying of God's only begotten Son.

During these excruciating moments the pain was more severe than any beating; more torturous than any crown of thorns; it was more humiliating than His nakedness; it was more ignoble than any Roman cross.

Jesus became sin.[83]

The Son of God who once lived in the pristine Holiness of unapproachable light was now assaulted by the storms of others transgressions; beaten by the tempest of this torture. In his utter aloneness for the first time in history, the anguish caused Him to cry out in abject isolation and pain unimaginable "My God, my God why have you forsaken me?" For the first time throughout all His humanity the Son of Man was alone, suspended between Heaven and Earth; or so He felt.

---

[82] Hebrews 10:20
[83] 2 Corinthians 5:21

The horror of this moment it too difficult for us to perceive, it will only be revealed in the eternals of Heaven how the fabric of eternity was stretched. It will only be in Heaven we will gain a glimpse of what it meant for Jesus to become sin for us. It will only be in the revelations of eternity that we will gain even a hint of what it might have been like for His God to turn His back upon the sin now placed upon this Son of Man. Our theology finds it a difficult concept to consider.

Soon after this horror, Jesus spoke again and said in **John 19:30** "It is finished." One word in the Greek – "tetelestai" – it means accomplished, finished, concluded, paid in full, over – it is finished!

After He made this pronouncement, the scripture says in **John 19:30**, "With that, he bowed his head and gave up his spirit." From the sidelines and still ignorant, Satan could barely believe his luck as he heard Jesus utter His last words; "It is finished."

It was one word that signified that the sufferings and agonies in redeeming mankind were over. One word that proclaimed the work long contemplated, long promised, long expected by prophets and saints, and was then done. One word that indicated to all of Heaven and Hell the toils in the ministry, the persecutions and mockeries, the pangs of the garden, His isolation and betrayal, and the cross, were ended. The price has been paid and man is redeemed. What a wonderful declaration this was!

It is finished! The malice and enmity of his persecutors had now done their worst. It's over.

It is finished, that is, the counsel and commandment of his Father concerning his sufferings were now fulfilled and he took care to see every iota of it exactly answered.

Plain View

It is finished, that is, all the prophecies of the Old Testament, which pointed at the sufferings of the Messiah; they were accomplished and answered.

It is finished, that is, the shadows seen in the ceremonial law and all the Laws of Moses are now fulfilled and now abolished through His flesh. The substance of the Law has now come, and all the shadows are done away.

It is finished, that is, his sufferings were now over, both those of His soul and those of His body. The storm is over, the worst is past; all his pains and agonies are at an end, and He is to enter the joy set before him.

It is finished, that is, He had breathed his last, and now He is no more in this world. He surrendered His spirit to God and He died like every man who had gone before Him.

It is finished, that is, the work of man's redemption is now completed, at least the hardest part of the undertaking is over; a full satisfaction is made to the justice of God, Christ had now gone through with his work, and finished it. Finished; the anger and the judgement of God is finished, consumed by the death of Christ on the cross, it is fulfilled and satisfied.

It was at this moment in time, at the very second of death, that God the Father could take it no longer! He turned back towards His now dead Son and with a shout that shook the foundations of Heaven as nothing had since the very day of creation, God Himself cried out, "Atonement! Redemption! Forgiveness; the Lamb of God slain! His blood the purchase price for the sins of the world! PAID!" The very foundations of Earth shook at the voice of God!!

The Father turned back towards a hateful world that had rejected their Messiah and had just killed His only Son but He turned towards them now no longer in rage or anger but in that moment of justice complete, He performed a miracle of unexpected and awesome significance.

As the Father moved from His throne in Heaven to Earth, He wasted no time; He waited not a single moment longer. In His haste to move in justice complete, the heavens had shook and now the Earth shook, the dead in tombs were raised and it was with swift justice He tore the veil, the curtain in the temple, that separated man from His presence for so long.

He shouted throughout the heavens and the Earth. It was His voice that again shook the very foundations of all that was His domain, "The way is open, the way is open! Behold a new and living way. The curtain between us had been torn. The way is open."

The curtain that prohibited mankind from coming into the Father's holy presence; this veil was torn from top to bottom by the very hand of God Himself signifying that the wall of partition is taken down. It signified that through the broken body of Jesus, through His broken flesh, mankind could now come into God's holy presence. Through the torn flesh of His Son, mankind could now come before their Father. Israel would no longer need the services of a priest or of a mediator. There was no longer any need of animal sacrifices. Sin's consequences were met, justice had been served, and Jesus had paid the ultimate price for man's salvation!

The law of commandments contained in ordinances, the Mosaic economy was now fulfilled forever to make way for a better hope. In **1 Timothy 2:5-7**, the apostle declares through the corridors of Heaven, Hell and the Earth, "For there is one God and one mediator between God and men, the man Christ Jesus, who gave himself as a ransom for all men the testimony given in its proper time. And for this purpose I was appointed a herald and an apostle."

Now you understand my zeal, now you might be able to comprehend my passion – now you might be able to get a glimpse and see the reason why I am so committed to serve the purposes of God. Now you may understand my passion for souls, now you see why I am so motivated by the cause of Christ! It is no emotion; it is no sentiment but the justice of God that results in a passion so raw to go and tell the world.

He is Dead.
It was getting late that Friday afternoon; the Sabbath day was fast approaching so Jesus, along with the two thieves, were removed from their crosses.

The justice of God was satisfied; Jesus had finished His mission, man was now reconciled to God through His death on the cross – **Romans 5:10**, "... we were reconciled to him through the death of his Son" – but Jesus had not completed His assignment and neither had God concluded. There were still a few acts of this divine drama to be played out.

The scriptures say in **John 19:38-42**, "At the place where Jesus was crucified, there was a garden, and in the garden a new tomb, in which no-one had ever been laid. Because it was the Jewish day of Preparation and since the tomb was nearby, they laid Jesus there."

In the strange eeriness after Jesus' death, His disciples, still ignorant, were scattered and in disarray. Close family and friends were attending the burial proceedings conducted by Joseph of Arimathea. As they finished, a stone was rolled over the entrance of the tomb.

A Roman guard was placed over the burial site; they'd heard rumours. The sun had set, the Sabbath had begun, and a new court room drama was about to unfold. Unseen by human eyes there was spiritual bustle and supernatural activity taking place behind the mortal veil. If it be possible, let me pull back the fabric of this dimension and give you a glimpse of what was taking place...

I believe that scripture teaches that Christ after He gave His life for sin on Calvary's cross, He commenced His descent into Hell itself there, He speaks to the spirits in prison.[84]

In **Ephesians 4:8–10** it says, "This is why it says: "When he ascended on high, he led captives in his train and gave gifts to men." What does "he ascended" mean except that he also *descended to the lower, earthly regions*? He who descended is the very one who ascended higher than all the heavens, in order to fill the whole universe."

Aquinas wrote; "Christ descended to the souls of the patriarchs who had died under the law, to announce redemption as accomplished and to free them from the prison where they were confined."[85]

The Psalmist did prophecy in **Psalms 16: 10**, "... you will not abandon me to the realm of the dead, [Sheol] nor will you let your faithful one see decay." The psalm doesn't say He would be spared a trip to the realms of the dead but that He would not be abandoned there!

The *Apostles' Creed* says, "... [Jesus was] crucified, dead, and buried; He descended into Hell. The third day He arose again from the dead..."

It was the fate of all human kind to experience death in this way; Jesus went the way of all who had died before Him. Remember the words of Jesus to the thief upon the cross (**Luke 23:43**) "Jesus answered him, "I tell you the truth, today you will be with me in paradise."

Jesus Christ's mission in descending to the lower earthly regions was not to just "taste death" like every person who had died before Him; but He was on a mission to also confront Satan, confront the

---

[84] 1 Peter 3:18-19 says, "He was put to death in the body but made alive by the Spirit, through whom also he went and preached to the spirits in prison."
[85] ft435 Aquinas, *Summa Theol.* III. 52. 5:

dominion of Hell, to stare Death in the eyes and to rip the fangs from the jaws of Sin.

Remember these startling truths, as He commenced His walk through the dingy palace of Hades, He died as a substitute for Mankind. He did not die for His own sins. He was the sacrifice for the sins of the whole world, but He Himself was pure and unblemished, He was a man of virtue. He was an innocent man condemned to death.

Jesus needed to interview Death and interrogate Hell for they sought to illegally hold Him who had known no sin! The force of sin known to mankind since Adam's disobedience was to be confronted and defeated once for all. As one Righteous and Holy, Death had to now understand its legal position. Death would have no legal right over Him; Satan would have no judicial privileges over His body![86]

Though He had died, His body would not see corruption because Death had no officially authorized claim over Him. He died; He tasted death, and as **Hebrews 2:9** says, "He suffered death, so that by the grace of God he might taste death for everyone."

This was the reason for Heaven's gasp of pain and horror; an innocent man had died! He was one blameless who walked in integrity and holiness. He was a man who was without sin and had passed from life unto death.

Remember this; no man took Jesus' life;[87] He gave His life willingly over to death and committed His Spirit to be given to His Father in Heaven. Jesus laid down His life of His own accord. (I mean, was it possible for someone to kill Jesus? Just a ponder.)

---

[86] Acts 2:27
[87] John 10: 17-18

Never in all the history of mankind had a death like this ever occurred or even been contemplated! Sin and Death had reigned from Adam until this moment.[88] Never before had the Earth witnessed the death of a righteous man. Never had an innocent man ever died. Remember this, the death of Jesus Christ was the most unique death to have ever taken place in all the history of time on Earth!

Satan was the judicial adversary of mankind. From Adam's disobedience, the Devil had authority over men, he was the "power of this dark world", "the ruler of the spiritual forces of evil" in the world, he was the power "now at work in sinful men" [89] he was the being who accused mankind before God both day and night.

Satan was "the god of this world!" **2 Corinthians 4:4**

Satan, one of the original archangels, was created by God to be the worship leader of Heaven but he perverted his role and bent Heaven's worship towards himself; he did this to usurp God's position and become the object of Heaven's worship.

Satan was beguiling, beautiful beyond belief and puffed up with pride beyond all wonder. Bloated by arrogance, he thought he could initiate a rebellion in Heaven and for this sin he was unceremoniously cast from Heaven along with a third of the angels (those who had disobeyed with him); it was upon the Earth that they set up their headquarters.

After Adam's disobedience, sin went viral, infecting the human race and Satan became the possessor of the Keys of Death and Hell, and he held mastery of the domains of all the Earth. Sublime, wickedly transcendent and, though only a created being, Satan possessed the Earth as his kingdom. He was arrogance personified. Pride, conceit and egotism ruined a character formed in glory.

---

[88] Romans 5:14
[89] Ephesians 6:12

Plain View

Remember during the temptation of Christ in the wilderness the Devil offered Jesus all the Kingdoms of the Earth? He could because they belonged to him.[90] In all his pride, his haughtiness and his personal vanity, Satan had made a huge tactical error.

Blinded by his own self-importance and side-lined by his own arrogance, he had not taken into account the many prophecies and promises of a resurrection. In his own egotism and smugness he miscalculated, overlooking the fact that Jesus was a man without sin; morally pure. It never dawned upon the satanic mind that Jesus would be the first innocent man to descend into Hell and into his domain.

What the Devil had overlooked was that he would have no judicial sway over Jesus after death; he would not able to contain Him. No demonic dungeon would be able to hold Him. No hellish detention had yet been fashioned to embrace Him. Hell had never seen an innocent man walking its corridors... until NOW!

It was this Jesus, the sinless one, the Holy One, Christ, the Son of the Living God who had come now to walk for the first time down the concourse of Hell. He walked in authority and in kingly might and He moved with confident ease as the Light of the World and on that day He walked into the very throne room of Satan.

He was there to fulfil the very first prophecy ever spoken about Him as Messiah. According to **Genesis 3:15** the scripture so long ago foretold that Messiah would come and, though He would bruise His heel, He would crush the serpent's head.

It was at this moment of realization; it was at this flash clarity of insight that Satan cried out with an utter knowing. The fabric of Hell began to rupture. It was this instant as King Jesus walked into the throne room of Hell that Satan finally realized his own pride and that

---

[90] Read Luke 4

his absolute defeat was at hand. Had someone recorded the Devil's words it would have been something like, "Oh no! I am ruined!" These words were a perfect complement to the words of Jesus "It is finished!"

It was at this moment when Jesus came face to face with Lucifer, the Accuser of the brethren that the Devil discovered his plan had not been thought out well. It was at this moment when Satan's haughtiness was fully revealed and Jesus began to make His just demands upon a beast who had ruled over the lives of men from the beginning of human history!

Again, if this had been recorded for the big screen we would first see the steely eyes of our Saviour as He regarded Satan; no pity. Secondly, you would have heard these words, "I now demand from you the Keys of Death and Hell! I want them right NOW!"

The keys of Death and Hell were surrendered! Then Jesus ripped the sceptre of authority from Lucifer's now limp hands and it was then Jesus grabbed him by the scruff of his neck and threw him to the ground like a common criminal. This act of final victory was witnessed by the demon generals that surrounded the throne of Satan, and enacted before the Angels of Heaven now no longer weeping but cheering Him on.

In staggering relief, God His Father in Heaven watched as Jesus threw Satan to the ground and with His feet still bruised by crucifixion, crushed the head of Satan right there in his own royal throne room. Jesus destroyed the power of Hell, crushed the force of Sin and for all times shattered the sting of Death!

In the words of Reinhardt Bonnke, "On that day, Jesus gave the Devil permanent brain damage." In the words of Paul the Apostle, found in **Colossians 2:15**, Jesus "... *disarmed* the powers and authorities, he made a public spectacle of them, triumphing over them by the cross." [Emphasis added by me!] The saints in prison began to cheer and in His train He led captivity captive[91] – the justice of God fulfilled – righteousness triumphs over evil!

The consequences of this audacious act caused a second wave of quakes, though not quakes upon the Earth but quakes through the spirit world of Satan's empire and of his now defeated domain. Jesus was about to leave these dungeons of death. It is worth a moment's thoughtfulness that **Jesus would be the FIRST person to ever do so in the history of mankind.**[92]

Death could not hold Him; sin had no grip on Him who was sinless.

The very fabric of Hell was shaking; the constitution of Hades was now shuddering; Gehenna at its very foundations was in a tremor, the world of the dead, the subterranean retreat of all that is hellish was quavering in a spin. The grave, that place of unquenchable fire, was finally in a revolution from which it would never recover!

It was then Jesus began to shout the prophecy of Hosea[93] also recorded in **1 Corinthians 15:54-57**, "Death has been swallowed up in victory." "Where, O death, is your victory? Where, O death, is your sting?"

Legally, Satan had no judicial rights over Jesus and for this reason He was able to secure victory for us all. Christ's mission was to rip from the hands of Death and Hell the right to rule and reign over those who would identify with the atoning death of Christ. Anyone who would identify themselves with His death would have absolute victory over all the powers of Hell. To even the weakest saint upon His knees every force of darkness was now defeated!

---

[91] Ephesians 4:8 - KJV
[92] 1 Corinthians 15: 20, 23
[93] Hosea 13:14

It is this victory that gave Jesus the right to powerfully declare in **Revelation 1:18**, "**I was dead and behold I am alive for ever and I hold the keys of death and Hades.**" It was this victory here that was to every believer the authority to declare: "Greater is he that is in you, than he that is in the world." **1 John 4:4** (KJV)

As this legal drama continued to unfold, Jesus began his triumphant march from Satan's throne room to experience, as no man had ever experienced, His resurrection from death. In a moment of self-realization, Jesus began to sense something of great power was now taking hold of Him. A transformation was beginning to take place! He had delivered those who were captive; He was victorious over Death and Hell. The power of sin, trounced.

Without thought to space and time, the Lord Jesus was instantly translated from Hades back to the tomb in which He had been laid. He knew this power, it was familiar to Him. He knew the promises of God. He knew what was about to take place. He knew He was about to be catapulted back from the dark domain of death and the grave.

He knew this was the power of God through the agency of the Holy Spirit.

Early that Sunday morning....
Early on the day after the Sabbath, a miracle so powerful occurred that we are not yet able to fully define its proportions; we have no words to describe it appropriately. It is indescribable!

There was the exertion of a power so great, a power so creative, and a power so magnificent, so glorious, so remarkable it left Hell in total disarray and has Earth still reeling!

This act of power resounded throughout the Earth and echoed through the courts of God in Heaven and ended as a shriek in the disarrayed courts of Hell. This release of power touched history by the creative act of God Almighty.

God had raised Jesus His Son from the dead by the power of the Holy Spirit and in doing so gave the gift of eternal life to everyone who would now believe upon Him.

This was the beginning of a new era for the universe, the decisive turning-point for the human race. In the resurrection, a new age had arrived, and this stupendous miracle signified the storming of history and the transforming of the world. The Resurrection was evidence that there had now appeared, in the midst of time, life of a new dimension and a promise of eternity.

The Resurrection: Central to all of Theology
Many people focus on the death of Christ as the central doctrine of the Church but it is the resurrection that is the central piece of doctrine to the Christian Church. The impact of the resurrection cannot be overstated or overrated. Never overstated!

The resurrection of Jesus Christ is THE most stupendous act of God's grace. It is the focal point of all human history. It is the transforming reality in light of which everything else must be interpreted. All meaningful human existence must be interpreted by the Earth-shattering, death-defeating, history-defining reality of Jesus' resurrection.

Christianity is not a message of merely what "has been" (past) and "will be" (future); it is the message of what "is" the vital dynamic of the resurrected Jesus who restores the whole of creation. The Resurrection facilitates and is the personal dynamic of the restoration of humanity whereby God functions once again in man by the presence of His own divine life in the Christian. Christ's life is ours by vital union with Him, and because He lives, we shall live also.

God's plan of salvation was set; it was in the inscrutable wisdom of God that the resurrection had to happen. The resurrection of Christ was to be God's "Amen" to Christ's "It is finished!"

In Peter's first sermon on the Day of Pentecost he said; "But God raised him from the dead, freeing him from the agony of death, because it was impossible for death to keep its hold on him." **Acts 2:24**

Paul opens a letter to the Romans with these words; "... regarding his Son, who as to his human nature was a descendant of David, and who through the Spirit of holiness was declared with power to be the Son of God, by his resurrection from the dead: Jesus Christ our Lord." **Romans 1:3-4**

1 Corinthians 15:3-4 says "For what I received I passed on to you as of first importance: that Christ died for our sins according to the Scriptures, that he was buried, that he was raised on the third day according to the Scriptures."

Apart from the resurrection there is no Christianity. Apart from the Resurrection there is no gospel. Apart from the Resurrection there is no spiritual life. Apart from the Resurrection there is no salvation. Apart from the Resurrection there is no righteousness, holiness or godliness. Apart from the Resurrection there is no Christian living. Apart from the Resurrection there is no hope.

Here is the truth and it's not out there – it's right here right now: Jesus Christ was raised from Death by the power of the Holy Spirit. He lives today and His resurrection power is available to all who would call upon His name. It is an energy whose source is in God; it comes from deep Heaven and was prescribed before eternity.

If the resurrection is the most stupendous act of God in all of recorded History (and it is!) then the close second is the salvation of one soul! The resurrection opened the door for mankind to experience eternal life with Christ; here and now and forever after the death of our physical bodies.

The Message puts **Ephesians 1:20 – 23** this way; "All this energy issues from Christ [when] God raised him from death and set him on a throne in deep heaven, in charge of running the universe. He is in charge of it all, has the final word on everything and at the centre of all this, Christ rules the Church. [A] Church not peripheral to the world but a world peripheral to the Church. The Church is Christ's body, in which he speaks and acts, by which he fills everything with his presence."

It is Christ's Church moving in an energy derived from the resurrection, a power touching a world with miracles and salvation. A Church so passionate that now – not even the gates of Hell can stop it – a Church so expansive with energy that not even the gates of Hell will be able to keep it out!

Jesus Christ: Radical Beyond Measure

Part Three: The Ascended Christ – Apocalypse RIGHT NOW!

The greatest danger for most of us is not that we aim too high and we miss it, but we aim too low and reach it. **Michelangelo.**

The Lord ate from a common bowl, and asked the disciples to sit on the grass. He washed their feet, with a towel wrapped around His waist - He, who is the Lord of the universe! **Titus Flavius Clemens (c.150 - c. 215), also known as Clement of Alexandria.**

Chapter 7: John on Patmos - not the Jesus I thought I knew!

The year was 95AD. The Apostle John, one of the original twelve disciples (also known as "the disciple whom Jesus loved") has been convicted and exiled to a remote desert island penal colony. The place of his deportation was an inaccessible Greek island by the name of Patmos.

The Roman emperor of this time, Titus Flavius Domitianus (also known as known as **Domitian**), had sentenced John to exile on the island because of his incessant and relentless preaching of Jesus. John's preaching had become a direct challenge to the worship of the emperor, and like Jesus, John was upsetting other religions and, from Domitian's perspective, needed to be silenced.

In the mind of Domitian, John was dangerous; he was dangerous to the Roman Empire, dangerous to civil peace and prosperity and he was dangerous in his undermining the plethora of other religions that were all the rage in the day.

The brand of religion John was peddling had turned out to be very popular, it was growing so quickly and it was having a profound and, in the mind of Domitian, very destabilizing impact on people, society and his policies. For Domitian, John was a very dangerous man to have walking around the place!

Patmos was the perfect place for him; it was a quarry mine and home to some of the Roman Empire's worst and most unpleasant prisoners. His fellow prisoners would be murderers, killers and some of the nastiest individuals the world could dredge up. History tells us that John was accompanied by Prochorus, his trusted scribe and servant.

Patmos was the Alcatraz of John's day; it was a desperate place for desperate men. It was a place from which no prisoner had ever escaped; and to be honest, none even thought about escape! This concept was not lost on John and his trusted servant either; this was going to be the place of his death – or so he thought.

The Lord's Day
As a Christ follower, John was dedicated to his worship of Jesus as God's Son. It was just like yesterday he remembered Jesus' ascension back into Heaven and the coming of the Holy Spirit.

For John, Jesus was ever alive within his own spirit and every Sunday, regardless of his geography and civil situation, John would conduct a worship service and speak to any who would listen. It just so happened he was now on Patmos; and nothing had changed his convictions, his plans or his passions.

Everyone remembers; John was a dangerous man! What did he care if his congregation this morning was made up of rapists, thieves, murderers and other civil dissidents! The simple fact that John was on Patmos AS A PRISIONER was evidence enough for the other prisoners to hold him in some kind of "criminal respect"!

As history tells us, John would find himself each Sunday - the Lord's Day - in a small grotto, like a natural amphitheatre of stone. It was here that he would sing psalms and spiritual songs to His Saviour and Redeemer. He would preach Jesus and open the word of God; invariably men would come to faith in Christ.

Patmos, far from being his prison, became a place to win men to Christ; many of these hardened criminals turned from their unbelief and responded to his preaching and embraced Christ. The story was

Plain View

repeated by all of the other Disciples of Christ too; in their imprisonment they were also able to lead not only prisoners but prison guards to faith in Christ. The popular apostle was once again a humble pastor; and loving it!

No Stranger

Even after seventy years, since Jesus had ascended into Heaven, John was still as passionate about Jesus as ever; more passionate actually! John was no stranger to Jesus; after all he was the disciple "whom Jesus loved"![94] John had spent time with Jesus – three years as a matter of fact. If anyone knew Jesus, John did.

John, the youngest of the disciples, had been there from the beginning. He had seen Jesus do so many things. His gospel account is replete with miracles, authoritative sermons and potent encounters with demonic forces. John knew Jesus.

John had seen Jesus calm the Sea of Galilee, turn water into wine, heal blind people and raise others from the dead. John watched in horror as Jesus engaged in conversation with that woman from Samaria who was of some dubious moral standing; did He have no sense of propriety? All He wanted was a drink of water. There was no need for engaging in conversation; she was a woman, a Samaritan and immoral! Jesus was sometimes crazy; caring very little for convention. John had a quiet laugh to himself!

John was no stranger to Jesus; he was both enamoured with Jesus and at times frightened by Him. John no doubt loved Jesus, it was undeniable, but sometimes he thought Jesus was "round the bend", maybe even a bit unbalanced. Jesus didn't act like other Rabbis or teachers of the Law, He spoke with an authority that grabbed people's attention, but He was wild and at times unpredictable. No one ever spoke like Him!

---

[94] John 13:23

John knew Jesus and had seen His power and had witnessed His authority. John was there when their boat landed on the forsaken coast line of Gadara where a man possessed by a legion of demons came running towards Jesus. For John, it was one of the most frightening and terrifying days of his life with Jesus!

The demon possessed man was naked, dirty, and unkempt with his beard and his hair long in tatters. The chains others had used to confine him were whipping around dangerously... and he was running full pelt towards them; Jesus just stood there.

You could hardly believe your eyes or your ears. The man came running towards them shrieking and shouting abuse and then quite suddenly, threw himself at Jesus' feet. A hideous voice spoke from out of the man. Jesus conducted a very short and sharp dialogue with the evils spirits inside this desperate man and then ordered them out of the poor soul.

John was there to watch as His Messiah stood His ground and called the demons out of that poor, wretched man and commanded those demons into a herd of pigs. It was the stuff of nightmares as the ear shattering squealing was only broken when the entire herd of frenzied pigs ran down the embankment and drowned. It was one of the most chilling moments of John's life in following Jesus.

Later that very day the man who had terrified a whole city was now clothed and in his right mind; what could be said, the disciples were all simply stunned!

John knew Jesus; he watched as Jesus went berserk one day in the Temple. John saw Jesus make a whip of cords and started hitting the animals and driving them out of the Temple. He turned the tables over on the money changers; it was a frightening thing to behold.

John knew Jesus; and, if the truth be told, feared for Jesus' life. He was sure that on that day in the Temple someone was going to kill

Plain View

Him right there on the temple forecourt! But as per usual he was dumbfounded as Jesus calmed everyone and sat down and started teaching the gathering crowd like nothing had happened.

It sometimes appeared to John that Jesus had a death wish, the way He went at things! One day, Peter tried to convince Jesus to relax and convince him that whatever He was to do, not to go to Jerusalem because they were going to kill Him; it earned Peter an awful rebuke. Jesus said to Peter "get behind me Satan!"[95] John wondered would Peter just go; but He didn't – none of them could! Jesus was different; He was scary, awe inspiring and downright dangerous; but each them they knew He was different. He alone had the message of eternal life! He was the Christ!

John was no stranger to Jesus; he witnessed first-hand the aggressive encounters that Jesus had with the religious leaders of their day. He heard the words of stinging criticism. He watched the faces of the priests twisting with embarrassment and anger as Jesus spoke to them.

John watched as Jesus blatantly broke their understanding of Sabbath laws to heal those in such extreme need. For Jesus it seemed that rules were just for breaking! John knew Jesus had compassion but saw that His tactics caused those religious leaders to become angry and furious; John watched as they conspired to murder Him.

John knew Jesus; the revolutionary and reformer. John had heard how Jesus told stories about despised Samaritans, making them the heroes of his story to the utter shock and irritation of the Pharisees; and John saw they hated Jesus for it. John watched fascinated as this revolutionary rabbi from Nazareth attracted crowds of common everyday people; and he saw they loved Him.

---

[95] Matthew 16: 23 and Mark 8:33

Jesus was irresistible! It was just something about Him. He embodied something totally unique, it was unfathomable. He was different!

John had heard the sermon where Jesus said people had to drink His blood and eat His flesh if they wanted to follow Him. He saw people offended and walk away; he wanted to as well but something compelled him to stay with Jesus. He was uncommon!

John saw Jesus hold children and bless them. John watched as Jesus wept for a friend at his funeral; he then watched Him raise His friend to life again four days after he died! John saw Jesus feed five thousand people with a little boy's lunch! John watched, deeply touched, as Jesus responded with so much compassion to that woman with the issue of blood; Jesus called her daughter and immediately she was healed!

John knew Jesus; it was John at supper who lent in close and rested his head upon His chest and quietly questioned Him concerning his betrayal. John loved Jesus. Jesus loved John too.

John knew Jesus and was familiar with His agenda. It scared John; he was only a young man!

John was there when Judas, who was one of their own, betrayed Jesus with a kiss in the garden. It was sheer horror! How could Judas have done such a thing? What was he doing? Why? But deep down John understood; Jesus was God's son who had come to die for the sins of the world. Deep down He knew Jesus was going to die in Jerusalem.

John was there when Jesus was taken away for judgement by the temple guards. John was there when Jesus was beaten, spat upon and ultimately nailed naked to a wooden cross.

John was the only one of the disciples who was present at the crucifixion of His Lord. He watched the suffering and the pain; many times that day he wished he could have looked away but he didn't. On that day he cried; he cried so much he wondered if he would ever cry like that again. John loved Jesus.

John was there with Mary, Jesus' mother, and some of the other women and John heard every last word Jesus ever said while on His cross; and John saw Jesus die. He would never get that image out of his head.

John was no stranger to Jesus; he heard and agreed with the Roman Centurion who spoke at the death of Christ and said, "Truly this man was the Son of God[96]."

He finally understood! John now KNEW Jesus; it all came into focus.

It was only a few days later when John saw, with immense joy, the resurrected Christ. John was astounded when he was able to touch Him, hold him and have Him close once again. Though His body still bore the scares of His passion, John knew this was Jesus; his Jesus and his Lord.

John was no stranger to Jesus; he had been at all the meetings Jesus had with everyone during the forty days Jesus was still on Earth. They marvelled at the dynamic of His new resurrected body! It was true; Jesus was the Son of God. He was Messiah!

John was there when Jesus breathed on them and said "Receive the Holy Spirit."[97] – John's eyes were further opened – He knew Jesus and would follow Him for the rest of his life!

John was there when Jesus ascended into the heavens too; that day was indelibly etched in his memory. John also heard Him say he

---

[96] Mark 15:39
[97] John 20:22

would be back! John knew first-hand Jesus Christ and worshipped Him as Messiah.

John was present on the day of Pentecost when the Spirit of Christ was poured out upon the Church. Glorious was that day as they were clothed with power from the ascended Christ. John spoke in tongues as the Spirit of Christ gave him utterance; John sensed a new anointing of power that day!

John had a deep and abiding sense he was called to further the knowledge of Christ throughout the world.

John saw Peter preach the first sermon and witnessed as three thousand people made a commitment to Christ; John was alive when Peter was killed by the Roman government but by then was a target himself – Rome hated him as they had hated Jesus.

For over seventy years John was active as a preacher, theologian and leader in the Church. He had travelled far and wide preaching the message of Jesus Christ. He met Paul, once known as Saul, and it was like hanging out with Jesus all over again. Paul was crazy! He preached long sermons and stirred up whole cities as he declared the power of Jesus Christ. John heard when Paul was killed too and he wept at such a loss to the Church.

John, for some reason, just outlived all of the other disciples and at the age of ninety was really old when the government of Rome decided to arrest and exile him to the island prison of Patmos. "That's it," he thought; "I'm finished."

John knew Jesus; personally and intimately. But John was totally unprepared for the revelation he was to receive on Patmos that day. The vision blasted John out of the water!

Never before had he seen such a picture of Jesus – John knew Jesus but had never seen His Lord so crowned with honour and glory! If John had known fear when Christ stilled the storm and cast out

Plain View

demonic spirits, John was now in absolute and total holy terror and in a deathly dread as he now confronted this vision of His Lord and King... and friend.

This vision of Jesus would have eternal consequences for John and thankfully for the Church for the next 2,000 years! It was this vision that added to his lifelong knowledge of Christ that would keep the Church alive and propel it into the world for the next 2,000 years and beyond.

Tom Rawls

This book had to be written by one of three people: good men, bad men or God. It couldn't have been written by good men because they said it was inspired by the revelation of God. Good men don't lie and deceive. It couldn't have been written by bad men because bad men would not write something that would condemn themselves. It leaves only one conclusion. It was given by divine inspiration of God. **John Wesley, British religious leader who founded Methodism (1703-1791).**

They gave him a manger for a cradle, a carpenter's bench for a pulpit, thorns for a crown, and a cross for a throne. He took them and made them the very glory of his career. **W.E. Orchard, Catholic author.**

Chapter 8: The Ascended Christ - Radical Beyond Measure

Giotto di Bondone (1266/7 – 1337) was an Italian painter and architect from Florence. He is generally considered the first in a line of great artists who contributed to the Italian Renaissance. His biography is first in Vasari's book on the *Lives of the Artists*.

His now famous work, *The Ascension,* adorns the Scrovegni Chapel (or Cappella degli Scrovegni) also known as the "Arena Chapel", a church in Padua, Veneto, Italy. The fresco is an outstanding example of the first of the Renaissance artists seeking to reveal the potency and power of the ascended Christ.

John records this experience in his letter *The Revelation of Jesus Christ* one Sunday while imprisoned on Patmos:

On the Lord's Day I was in the Spirit, and I heard behind me a loud voice like a trumpet, which said: "Write on a scroll what you see and send it to the seven Churches: to Ephesus, Smyrna, Pergamum, Thyatira, Sardis, Philadelphia and Laodicea.

I turned round to see the voice that was speaking to me. And when I turned I saw seven golden lamp stands, and among the lamp stands was someone "like a son of man", dressed in a robe reaching down to his feet and with a golden sash round his chest. His head and hair were white like wool, as white as snow, and his eyes were like blazing fire. His feet were like bronze glowing in a furnace, and his voice was like the sound of rushing waters. In his right hand he held seven stars, and out of his mouth came a sharp double-edged sword. His face was like the sun shining in all its brilliance.

When I saw him, I fell at his feet as though dead. Then he placed his right hand on me and said: "Do not be afraid. I am the First and the Last. I am the Living One; I was dead, and behold I am alive forever and ever! And I hold the keys of death and Hades. "Write, therefore, what you have seen, what is now and what will take place later." **Revelation 1:10-19**

Majestic and stately is this picture of the now ascended Christ. Frightening and yes, even terrifying was His countenance. It had been over seventy years since John had seen His Lord; and Jesus was now standing right before him!

Yes, he walked with Christ. He knew the presence of Christ and heard His voice day by day! But this was different; like at the resurrection but totally, absolutely and incredibly different.

His face, His voice, His eyes! Never before had Jesus ever shown Himself to John in this manner. Absolute fearsome terror gripped John and when Jesus reached out His hand to touch him, he fell down before Him like a dead man! Such was the impact, the shock and the impression His presence and the vision had upon John.

John, the disciple whom Jesus loved, had never seen His master in such a light. This life sentence of incarceration and probable death had been transformed into a most holy encounter with Jesus Christ who was describing Himself as the "First and the Last, the Living One, who was dead and behold he is alive for ever more; He who hold the keys of death and Hell!"

What a mind blowing encounter! This would have been a life changing experience for John, an already frail man in his nineties, close to the end of his life. It was a fresh and potent revelation of the ascended Christ; John had never seen Jesus in such fierce majesty!

This was no vision of a "gentle Jesus meek and mild"[98] surrounded by laughing children; His eyes were like fire and sword protruded from His mouth. I am sure children may have been frightened if they saw Jesus like this.

This was no Jesus seated on a donkey receiving accolades from a crowd either. No, this revelation of Christ had Him seated on a white horse, feet red hot like burnished bronze and a face that shone like the noon day sun; blinding in its brilliance.[99]

The First Century Christ for a 21st Century Church
This record of the revelation of Jesus Christ is forever recorded, bursts with inspiration and remains a stimulus to the Church today. This first century picture of the ascended Christ recorded here by John in the book of Revelation must be added to the foundations of our 21st century Church and our mission into the entire world. It is the only record of a vision of the ascended Christ found in scripture. This book abounds in an intimate and yet life shattering revelation of the ascended Christ.

We need to read and reread this book! If only to receive the blessing attached; **Revelation 1:3**: "Blessed is the one who reads the words of this prophecy, and blessed are those who hear it and take to heart what is written in it, ***because the time is near***." (Emphasis added)

To build 21st century churches we continue to need a bold, powerful and overwhelmingly fresh vision of, and intimate encounters with, Jesus Christ.

---

[98] Poem by Charles Wesley
[99] Revelation 1:15

This is Jesus who is described in these passages as "the faithful witness, the firstborn from the dead, and the ruler of the kings of the earth"[100]; "the One who loves us and has freed us from our sins by his blood". [101]

This is the Christ who declares "I am the Alpha and the Omega [the One] who is, and who was, and who is to come; the Almighty."[102] His bold and triumphant announcement is that He is the First and the Last."

But wait ... He's not finished: He cries out with such a loud voice and in doing so rips the very fabric of all time and eternity to say "I am the Living One; I was dead, and behold I am alive forever and ever! And I hold the keys of death and Hades."[103]

"I am alive forever and ever!"

These radical depictions of the ascended Christ recorded here in Revelation are central to the formation of our ecclesiology and pivotal to the core of our missiology. Without these clear pictures of Jesus we will never build a Church that reaches the world, bringing them to an allegiance with the One and True God.

Without a completed vision of Christ, there will be no lasting impact on the lives of those who are called to bow their knee to the ruler of the kings of the Earth. **John 17:3** puts it this way: "Now this is eternal life: that they may know you, the only true God, and Jesus Christ, whom you have sent."

In this vision recorded by John we see a Jesus who is no longer the "baby Jesus", harmlessly held to the virgin's breast. He is no longer a teenage child held in awe by religious leaders for His astute insight

---

[100] Revelation 1:5
[101] Revelation 1:5
[102] Revelation 1:8
[103] Revelation 1:17-18

and profound understanding. He is not just a revolutionary and reformer criticising the religious leaders of His day; he is not just a miracle worker and sage prophet. He is seen as more than just a compassionate healer and a friend of sinners.

This is no longer the picture of the suffering saviour of the world, hanging naked on a cross but a Jesus who has broken through the bonds of Hell and Death to now reign in unimaginable authority as the ascended ruler of the kings of all the Earth; the very central figure of our faith and loyalty.

John looked on in awe and saw this vision of Christ. His last book, *The Revelation of Jesus Christ*, has a number of these paradigm altering pictures of Christ which are there to impact our 21st century world and our attempts at re-presenting Him.

The Vision
"I was there on the Lord's Day, in the Spirit and I was worshipping Jesus – I was singing this song and I heard a voice behind me it sounded like a trumpet!"[104]

Volume
I am continually overwhelmed by how loud Jesus is! It almost seems like after a few years Church folk developed sensitive ears and love the quiet and hushed tones of worship. Where did this need for quiet reflection come from? For someone like me, the quintessential 21st century man, "I like my music and I like my music LOUD!"

What has happened to our churches when we can't express our passions, our enthusiasm or our intensity? What's with all this quietness? Tip toeing around God's house is not good. Jesus spoke and His voice was LOUD like a trumpet!

---

[104] Revelation 1:10

'Quiet as a church mouse', the saying goes... Can you believe people go to sleep in church? I know we sometimes preach for hours and little children get tired and teenagers can fall from balconies[105] but where did it originate that we were to present Jesus as quiet, nervous and a bit jumpy? Where did it come from that churches were supposed to be quiet places where you speak in serious and hushed tones? I just don't get it. Who started this evil rumour?

Jesus speaks with a loud voice for our world today that is awash in media white noise, inundated with tens of thousands of commercials and the commotion of living in such an age. We need a commanding voice to make an impression and cut through the crap!

John said, "I turned to look and I saw..."

Lamp stands: LIGHT
Seven golden lamp stands, and among the lamp stands was someone "like a son of man." The lamp stands are the churches specifically spoken of in this passage but the message is applicable it to all churches. I find it outstanding that the Church is referred to as a golden lamp stand. See the value placed upon her, she is "golden".

She is a lamp stand; she brings light to the world! She shimmers and illuminates. She is the Church; bright, creative, original and simply stunning. This church stands in stark contrast to the dry and dead burnt out husks of ancient building studding the cities and villages of Europe; beautiful architecture but many are just full of dead men's bones!

This startling vision has Jesus walking among the lamp stands. Now that's scary!! Jesus is walking around in the churches; moving about the place. It means He's here right now; walking amongst the people called His Church. It is His desire to presence Himself IN His Church.

---

[105] Acts 20:9-10

Plain View

The implication of this is not lost on the Church leaders; many struggle, in a good way, with what to do with Jesus as He moves IN His Church. For others it is a nightmare; "what do you do with Jesus as He moves IN His Church?"

But our 21st century world would be delighted to see Jesus moving IN and AROUND the place! It would be quite innervating and exciting for them in terms of sustaining an authentic faith. It's HIS Church and as leaders we need to ask Him way more often what He wants to do today.

His Robe

The vision goes on to describe Jesus Christ; He was dressed in a robe reaching down to his feet. This is a robe of righteousness and virtue.

Righteousness is a moral attribute of Christ; it also speaks of His justice. He is completely clothed down to His feet with this garment. Jesus is without sin or guilt and there is a sense of rightness about all of His actions and with Him as a person; with Him there is a sense of propriety. It is because of this righteousness we can trust Him to do whatever it is in His heart to do IN His Church.

His righteousness is complete and total; everything He does is in line with this absolute righteousness. This is no mini skirt of righteousness, this is full on down to the ground justice, righteousness and integrity, baby!

This righteousness is the self-imposed constraint He places upon Himself to only act righteously and just as the robe reaches to His feet it completely covers His body, Jesus rules in unquestionable righteousness, complete in every way.

There is no shadow of turning, no duplicity, no favouritism, and no partiality. He is utterly righteous and always acts justly! Justice is in His hands!

A Golden Sash

He stands with a golden sash round his chest. Normally a sash of this kind would be leather and worn around the waist to girt or dress a man for battle; not so with Jesus' sash. This sash is golden and has been placed upon the chest signifying a battle complete!

This sash is a symbol of His total and unconditional victory over all His enemies. It's signifies a battle won. There are none who can stand before Him. He has conquered and He has defeated every enemy; including Death and Hell.

He stands as the Living One who has met Death and Hell and who now rules with supreme authority and power. He has vanquished every adversary and there are no rivals! Victory, authority and power are His. No demonic force can stand against Him; no power of degenerate men can overcome Him – He is victorious overall and supremely triumphant. He is sovereign, the ruler of the kings of the Earth and supreme – no power can come against Him and win. No longer does He appear as safe, de-clawed and domesticated; this is not the gelded or sterile version of Jesus we have been fed for so long!

With this vision we find that Jesus is unable to fit into any of our pre-packed Sunday school pictures. There is no flannel graph for this picture, no stained glass rendition of Him for our devotion. Jesus stands before John looking quite dangerous, wildly passionate and incomparable in His authority and power.

Yet in the world around us we see that Jesus has restrained Himself in line with His character to not abuse His authority. Even though His is the ultimate authority in all the Earth he constrains Himself to act within the realm of His nature.

In our tech savvy world of video gaming and "man movies" guys especially are looking for a Jesus like this. When you compare

Leonidas[106] of the movie *300* with the flannel graph pictures of Jesus you just feel a little ripped off.

His Head and Hair

His head and hair were white like wool, as white as snow. This picture exposes yet another attribute of Christ; His eternity. White hair speaks of old age or advanced years but who could ever attribute age to our Lord Jesus?

Jesus Christ is ageless, timeless and He lives in eternity where time has no sway. He stands before John as the God Eternal.[107] Isaiah calls Him the 'Rock eternal'.[108] Daniel speaks about Him being the King of an eternal kingdom![109]

Without this book of Revelation we wouldn't have such a clear picture of the eternity of Christ or have so developed the whole concept of eternity for the Church. Jesus is certainly eternal and the book of Revelation in chapter twenty-two explains for us what Heaven will be like and that we will live there with Christ forever.

His reign will never end. His influence will never cease. In triumphal benediction, Paul saw his glory and wrote; "Now to the King eternal, immortal, invisible, the only God, be honour and glory forever and ever. Amen.[110]" There will be no end to His rule! The impact of this truth is staggering when we consider it; it has an amazing bearing on our relationship with Christ and our destiny!

---

[106] Leonidas was a hero-king of Sparta, the 17th of the Agiad line, one of the sons of King Anaxandridas II of Sparta, was believed, in mythology, to be a descendant of Heracles, possessing much of the latter's strength and bravery. He is notable for his leadership at the Battle of Thermopylae.

[107] Genesis 21: 33

[108] Isaiah 26:4

[109] Daniel 4:3

[110] 1 Timothy 1:17

This eternal Christ must be revealed to a waiting world. If made known in this way we will find our desires for fictional places like Pandora will fade back to 2D and black and white and the fullness of all of Heaven will become our focus. We will no longer desire a world populated by skinny vampires who twinkle in the sunlight or yearn for bulky muscled dudes who can shape shift and transform into wolves if we can see this Jesus Christ in all of His triumph.

His Eyes

When John saw the eyes of the ascended Christ they were like blazing fire. These were NOT "Bette Davis eyes[111]!" They weren't Tay Tay's "Beautiful Eyes"[112] either – these were eyes of terrifying fire!

This vision must have shocked John to his core; *his* Jesus had never looked like this. *His* Lord had never cast eyes on him like this ever before. Somewhere deep in John's heart he felt fear. Those eyes were looking straight through him. John felt transparent and incredibly vulnerable. These eyes of fire speak of Christ and His omniscience.

The eyes of the Lord look into the hearts of all men and He knows our deepest secrets. The scripture says "God knows everything about us and no secret is hidden"[113]; this is an attribute of deity! The miracle of omniscience is that Christ knows everything about us; He knows what we have done and what we will do and nothing can be concealed from Him.

Our deepest secret, our most hidden agendas and our every attitude and motivation are laid bare to Him. And he still loves us and showers His grace upon us. His power is constrained by His love and mercy for us as fallen beings living in a hostile world. His anger and judgement

---

[111] *Bette Davis Eyes* is a song made popular by the American singer-songwriter Kim Carnes. The song was written in 1974 by Donna Weiss and Jackie DeShannon.
[112] Taylor Swift "Beautiful Eyes" 2008
[113] Hebrews 4:13

were spent upon Calvary, these eyes carry nothing but love, compassion and grace.

These eyes burn with zeal and a wild sense of passion; these are the eyes of raw enthusiasm. John, who had spent a lifetime walking with Christ, living a life of passion and holiness found it difficult to not avert his eyes from these burning orbs of pure zeal. Passion, fire and zeal; this is what John saw in the eyes of Jesus. Our role in the 21st century Church is to reveal those eyes to a world living in a bland and, at times, artificial world.

His Feet
In the vision, John saw His feet were like bronze glowing in a furnace. John, as a young man had walked literally hundreds of miles with Jesus in sandaled feet. He had seen Jesus' feet countless times; hey wait ... John had washed those feet countless times as well. But John had never seen His feet like this before.

This picture exposes Jesus as Almighty. He is omnipotent and all powerful. This Jesus revealed to John that He has no problems walking where ever He desires, going where ever He decides. Jesus had no need to ask for permission or seek approval; if He so desired He could go anywhere! Jesus has no peers or colleagues, no rival; He has no equals. He stands alone in raw dominance; He is The Lord God Almighty.

No force on Earth or in Heaven has such power. There is no match to His strength, no equal to His ability and no counterpart for His supremacy. He is ALMIGHTY.

We see this utter disregard to power when He walked the Earth; He preached boldly and when they tried to take Him captive, he simply vanishes out of their presence! This same Jesus now appears unbeatable and now unmatched in every fight within the universe. He stands ever ready to crush any resistance.

This picture of Christ must have struck a chord of abject horror and fear into the leaders of the church when at one point Jesus is knocking on the door of the church of Laodicea! He could have smashed the door down and if He so desired, could have, by force, walked into the midst of the church; yet He stands like a guest waiting to be invited in. Such restraint in the midst of such omnipotence is frightening to say the least.

Our world looks on with pity as they watch a Church dying before their very eyes. It is now our responsibility to re-present to our world and our time not some castrated version of Christ, impotent and powerless but a Christ radical beyond measure. Our need is to re-present an awesome and fierce Jesus who stands in power; not some constrained and weird Mad Hatter.

His Voice

It is recorded here that John also heard His audible voice and it was like the sound of rushing waters. Have you ever been near a big waterfall? As you listen to the sound of the water it literally feels like it surrounds you. The attribute of Christ being revealed here is His omnipresence. He is everywhere!

The great miracle of omnipresence is not so much that God is just so big that there is not one place in the universe where He is not. But listen to this and allow our finite minds to contemplate this truth: All of God is everywhere! He lives in me and He lives in you! I am not inhabited with only a part of God; no, all of God lives within me.

Surrounded and even hounded by the ubiquitous presence of Christ, Jesus impresses us with His being. Persistent and unrelentingly, He pursues us with His love and concern for our lives; always seeking our redemption.

David understood this when he cried out to the Lord: "Where can I go from your Spirit? Where can I flee from your presence? If I go up to the heavens, you are there; if I make my bed in the depths, you are there. If I rise on the wings of the dawn, if I settle on the far side of the sea, even there your hand will guide me, your right hand will hold me fast. If I say, 'Surely the darkness will hide me and the light become night around me,' even the darkness will not be dark to you; the night will shine like the day, for darkness is as light to you." **Psalms 139:7-12**

I'm sure this truth was not lost on John either; Jesus had told them that as they were to go into all of the world and He would be with them always even until the ends of the Earth.[114] The writer to the Hebrews said that His presence would never leave or forsake us.[115] For John, this was a powerful truth as he stood on Patmos; the end of the Earth for him.

How is it that there are some of Christ's followers who "feel" a million miles away from Jesus? The answer is they walk by sight and not by faith. They put way too much stock into their feelings and emotions and little into their faith. Christ will never leave us or ever forsake us. He is always with us. He is with us as Saviour, Creator and King. Even when we don't feel His presence, we know He is with us.

What I like about this picture is that we're never alone. Christ is always with us; we take His presence within us into our world. He is never far away but always near. I don't need to go and find Him, He is with us always even to the end of the Earth. He is not a fanciful and precocious god who is fickle and capricious, but always consistent and dependable.

The Seven Stars
In his right hand he held seven stars. These seven stars are the ministers of His Church[116] and being in His hand speaks of His power over them, His intimacy with them and His ability to lead them, speak

---

[114] Matthew 28: 20
[115] Hebrews 13:5
[116] Revelation 1:20

to them and protect them. Being in His right hand speaks of His creativity that would flow through them; it speaks of the source of their giftedness.

In my book *Relentless,* I explore this subject a bit more. I propose that those who lead the Church must be those who have been set aside by the Holy Spirit and approved by others who are also leaders of the Church. In **Acts 13** we read the account of how Paul and Barnabas were set aside by the leaders of the Jerusalem Church. During a time of fasting and prayer, the Holy Spirit spoke in a way which was witnessed and accepted by those gathered that these two men were indeed "ministry gifts of Christ."

I've seen men and women who have been "ministry gifts of Christ"[117] and I have seen the "wannabes". In 2 Peter chapter 2, I read where the Apostle Peter refers to "false prophets" and "false teachers" - those who have desired the office but lack the calling, the appointment and anointing.

It is sad, indeed scandalous, to see these kinds of people seeking the offices of Christ when in fact they are not gifted to do so. I've seen them; some look weak and ineffectual, others strut like CEOs splashing money everywhere, trying to impress others. I've watched as they attract a certain amount of notoriety. My heart breaks for the people they fool.

Peter says in 2 Peter 2 that in the last days, these false leaders would appear and that we need to take care to recognise them. You'll recognise them by these things: "They will secretly introduce destructive heresies, even denying the sovereign Lord who bought them, bringing swift destruction on themselves. Many will follow their shameful ways and will bring the way of truth into disrepute. In their greed these teachers will exploit you with stories they have made up." (**2 Peter 2:1-3**)

---

[117] Ephesians 4:11

It is a high and holy calling to be in the hands of the ascended Christ. James says in **James 3:1,** "Not many of you should presume to be teachers, my brothers, because you know that we who teach will be judged more strictly." Why would anyone seek the position of being in His right hand if he or she were not ministers of Christ and the opposite is true woe to the one who would try to snatch a man or woman of God sheltered in the palm of the Saviours hand!"

It is *so* time to reveal to the world men and women of supernatural power walking in integrity and righteousness. It's time for God's servants to stand up and be counted, to be all we can be – supernatural flames of fire sitting in the right hand of the Lord Jesus Christ.

Sharp Two Edged Sword
John saw that out of his mouth came a sharp double-edged sword. This is of course the word of God which eternally proceeds from His mouth. But the vision struck John with an awful fear. John knew Jesus was the Word; Jesus was with God and was God. John stood transfixed by this vision of Christ before him, an image beyond His wildest imagination.

Hebrews 4:12-13 says, "For the word of God is living and active. Sharper than any double-edged sword, it penetrates even to dividing soul and spirit, joints and marrow; it judges the thoughts and attitudes of the heart."

The Word is inspired and "God breathed." His word is like food to our souls, it is sweeter than honey, His word is TRUTH with a capital "T" and His word is a lamp unto our feet. You can live by the word of God and you can trust it; it is the word of God. But John had never been subjected to such a personal vision of the Word of God before! John trembled.

This world is tired of the "New Age" gurus with their thinly veiled principles of life. People long to eat the real bread of life. They want to know the Word of God has a bit of bite with it as well. In our attempts of seeking to make Jesus more palatable, we've made Him as bland as the world round us.

As Christians we are different! We offer the alternative to mediocrity and a lack of seasoning to life. We are the salt of the Earth and we need to re-present a Jesus whose word has pizzazz. As we present the Bible, we need to do it with its cutting edges powerfully revealed; caution these edges are sharp.

His Face
Finally, John saw His face and records it was like the sun shining in all its brilliance. This speaks of God's moral attribute of holiness. This speaks of His perfection, both morally and in character. Jesus Christ is free from moral evil and set apart from all that is worldly. Can anyone imagine the impact of this holiness upon anyone whose desire is draw close to Him?

There are few words to describe this attribute of Jesus; John said "His face was like the sun shining in all its brilliance."[118] He is unprecedented in all of human history, He is lofty, high and lifted up, He is exalted, His throne is elevated above all, there is no God like our God and there is none to compare with Him. He is morally pure, the very essence of His being is perfection and excellence; He is "flawless, absolutely flawless"[119] in His Holiness.

Yet even in such a purity of total holiness he is at home with humanity. He finds us fascinating. He is quite fond of us and desires relationship and fellowship with us. Even though His face shines like the noon day sun, he is willing to live in the hearts of broken and fallen humanity.

---

[118] Revelation 1:16
[119] Lyrics from the band "The Ones."

Plain View

Though transcendent in His holiness, He does not turn His face from us in our times of loneliness, heartache or trouble. Though incomparable in purity, He feels at home with us as we struggle in our battles with our weaknesses and our failings. Even for those who have yet to turn their thinking around about Him, he'll still give love. How this world needs to hear this message of holiness at home with humanity! A story of a God who is totally perfect yet desires to reside within *us*, who are so far from perfection. Such grace; such wonder – oh what a great Jesus we serve! This is Jesus in all of His glory! Look full into His wonderful face![120] This is the ascended Christ who stands in incomparable glory.

So much more....
The Revelation of Jesus Christ does not stop at this first vision of the ascended Christ but pervades the writing of John through this book. Jesus is seen as never before. The Gospel accounts are not wrong, they are just not complete; the visions of John give us a fuller and more robust picture of Jesus.

The ascended Christ as seen in this last book of the Bible doesn't hold back either; in a powerful show of energy he speaks to seven churches to give instruction, warning and encouragement. Unafraid and unconcerned with politics, He speaks with the incisive manner of The Great Physician[121] checking the health of every church.

He shows Himself strong through the rest of this book; from His throne shining in glory He rules as the supreme leader; He is unassailable, irrefutable, invincible and totally incontrovertible. He is seated in unquestionable authority surrounded by lightning and a thunderous roar. An emerald like rainbow[122] encircles His throne and a sea of crystal glass is before Him.

---

[120] Helen H. Lemmel, 1922
[121] Hymn by John Stockton
[122] Revelation 4:3

There is worship and it will be like nothing else – when you have the time, read the passages found in Revelation 5: 9-14. Awesome is the only word to describe our response to Him and it will take eternity for us to ever exhaust ourselves of giving Him glory.

The book of Revelation finishes with an outstanding and unrivalled vision of Christ; **Revelation 19:11-16** says this: "I saw heaven standing open and there before me was a white horse, whose rider is called Faithful and True. With justice he judges and makes war. His eyes are like blazing fire, and on his head are many crowns. He has a name written on him that no-one knows but he himself. He is dressed in a robe dipped in blood, and his name is the Word of God."

"The armies of heaven were following him, riding on white horses and dressed in fine linen, white and clean. Out of his mouth comes a sharp sword with which to strike down the nations. 'He will rule them with an iron sceptre.' He treads the winepress of the fury of the wrath of God Almighty. On his robe and on his thigh he has this name written: KING OF KINGS AND LORD OF LORDS."

The essential teachings of Jesus... were literally revolutionary, and will always remain so if they are taken seriously. **Herbert Muller, American Historian.**

We've already opened the 21ˢᵗ century Danny. I think it's too late to send it back. **Lindsay Monroe, *CSI New York* (played by Anna Belknap.)**

Then their eyes were opened and they recognised him. **Luke 24:31.**

Many believe - and I believe - that I have been designated for this work by God. In spite of my old age, I do not want to give it up; I work out of love for God and I put all my hope in Him. **Michelangelo.**

Chapter 9: Audacious - Big - Bold - Potent - Wild - Jesus on Display

From Leonardo to Michelangelo, renaissance men painted religious scenes. Their subjects were angels and demons, "The Madonna and Child" and many of the saints. There was, of course, a prolific amount of works painted with the subject being Jesus; from childhood to crucifixion, from His transfiguration to His trials and tribulations and on to His ascension. They all made great art based on the person of Jesus.

The Da Vinci great would have to be *The Last Supper* or *Salvator Mundi* (Saviour of the World), while Michelangelo's great portrayals of Christ would be those on the ceiling of the Sistine Chapel. Raphael portrays Christ from his earliest work, from the *The Resurrection of Christ* (finished in 1502), to *Christ falling on the way to Calvary* (finished in 1517); his portrayals of Christ are awe inspiring and beautiful.

My concern with these renditions is that some of the artists make Christ look weak, emaciated and at times effeminate. Da Vinci's *Salvator Mundi* is probably the exception, showing the face of Christ in startling detail and, apart from a slightly ethereal touch, He looks manly and masculine! These pictures have been preserved through the centuries and have gone towards developing our picture of Jesus.

As much as I love these great Renaissance artists, and I do, I don't necessarily agree with their portrayal of Christ as fragile. Let me explain.

Why do we think Jesus was frail? Why is it that so many artists portrayed Him as slightly effeminate and with a really beautiful face? Why is He portrayed as a victim? Why do these painters try and make Him look less than muscular and robust? Is there something inheritably holy about being slight, thin and girly?

Why is Jesus never seen to smile or even look relaxed? Jesus appears ethereal, sort of otherworldly and a bit insubstantial in His delicacy. Why does he have a halo!?? Does this make Him look more godly or less human? What are they seeking to portray?

Yet Michelangelo did get humanity right with his statue of David. This statue engenders such commentary, and has done so for centuries. This masterpiece of Renaissance sculpture was created between 1501 and 1504 and stands 5.17 metres (17 foot)! Many are overwhelmed by its size and immediate impact. Others are embarrassed by the fact David is nude and some, more scholarly, comment on the fact that as a Jew he's not circumcised!

On the 8th September 1504, the statue of David was unveiled and placed outside the **Palazzo della Signoria** and only later moved to the Academia Gallery in Florence in 1873. I saw this immense work in 2016. The statue has inspired generations and motivated millions because of its beauty and strength.

David appears just like the hero of **1 Samuel 17**. He is portrayed by Michelangelo as strong, muscled, even chiselled (pun intended). He is handsome, masculine and appears confident and sure. I think it

Plain View

was a stroke of genius that Michelangelo made the statue of David appear to be the same size as what Goliath might have been in real life; David is massive and his very posture reveals his power.

Whatever Jesus looked like in the flesh, and I don't think He was as effeminate or girly looking as He was painted by the Renaissance artists, He is so much more than that!

Paul, in his writings to the Corinthian church, was quick to point out that though he had never seen Jesus "in the flesh" and that we should no longer consider Him merely from a fleshly or worldly perspective. **2 Corinthians 5:16-17** speaks clearly: "So from now on we regard no-one from a worldly point of view. Though we once regarded Christ in this way, we do so no longer. Therefore, if anyone is in Christ, he is a new creation; the old has gone, the new has come!"

No doubt Peter and the disciples were preaching up a storm where ever they went and would often tell stories of when they were with Jesus. I can just imagine Peter speaking to the crowd one Sunday and breaking into his story of walking on the water! The crowd would eat that stuff up. But just as important as it is to understand His earthly ministry, what He did and what He taught, we desperately need to see and understand that Jesus was crucified, died and rose again but that He lives forever in eternity according to the vision John articulated.

Even in His resurrected body and now ascended to Heaven, Jesus is still fully human and still the possessor of His divinity and according to **1 Corinthians 15:20** "... Christ has indeed been raised from the dead, the first fruits of those who have fallen asleep."

Paul's message and his preaching were not delivered in what would be regarded as persuasive or particularly articulate words. What he did know about Christ, he preached and employed the power of God in doing so.

He spoke to a Gentile audience who had no idea of who Jesus was but were bombarded by religious images regularly. His letter to the Corinthian church seemed to present Jesus powerfully! He had to bring the people of his day from a known to an unknown. He created visual bridges in preaching that caught people's attention and he firmly anchored them with spiritual power and a supernatural dynamic. He spoke from the perspective of their own secular prophets and linked them with the divine!

My premise is that here, in the new Western world, we have moved into a "pre-Christian" era. The Church no longer occupies a place of political power or moral command in the world around us. We can no longer thunder forth the Lord's declarations like the prophets of old. There are few who have the openings to walk into congress or parliaments and declare the word of the Lord. We can no longer legislate holiness through the courts, though we can have a level of influence. It seems the world is losing its grip upon the Judeo-Christian ethic that has driven the judicial system for centuries.

@JonnyMeah tweeted recently "... @tomrawls is it moral for St Paul's Cathedral to be charging admission fees? #mytwibate".

Is it moral? The situation is if they don't charge an admission fee, their cash flow would be in danger. The West is surrounded by the dying husks of dried out churches. Some would call them "glorious ruins."

Some of these buildings are indeed beautiful but the buildings constructed to house a move of God have now been turned into tourist attractions and mausoleums to house the dead. In many of these buildings, you literally walk over the tombs of dead people to get into the church.

Europe is troublingly reminded of its future as congregations are literally dying out and vanishing. On a recent BBC documentary concerning the nation of Finland, they were reporting that over one thousand Fins are leaving the traditional Church each week.

In the UK, the figure is a staggering two thousand a week leaving the Church and over one thousand of them are under twenty five, though some are suggesting there is a turn around. However, the aging membership of the Church is a very present concern as most communicants of the Church reach their eighties and nineties and prepare to die.

Out of the aftermath of dying churches, there rises - like a Phoenix from the ashes - a sleek, stunning and powerful Church; fresh with vision and creative in their presentation of Jesus Christ. Our work is to seek to build relationships with our world where we are then, hopefully, given permission to speak.

Some are irked by this thought of being given permission to speak; let me finish. Some in our society would honestly say the Church has no business being in business. Some are even angry with the Church and others out right antagonistic towards a supposed concept of a God.

Many, like Richard Dawkins, pay good money to launch their personal bus campaigns to say things like "There's probably no God." The Pope acknowledged that there was a dangerous atheism and aggressive secularism.

The atmosphere in the West is studded by a militaristic secular world view. It was in Europe that Darwin postulated his theories on evolution and for centuries now we have taught them in schools. Is it any wonder we have such a secular view of history and humanity? With an anti-god sentiment, segments of modern society are intentionally working towards a very liberal view of life and a matching lifestyle.

For many, Jesus Christ is ignored and in a lot of places His name remains just a swear word. Few would consider a personal relationship with Him. Some might say He was a good man but few would pledge their loyalty towards Him; fewer still would be willing to die for Him. Even those who are Christians, at times, feel ambivalent towards Christ and His command over their lives.

So my effort is to prayerfully enlist the person of the Holy Spirit to assist me to raise the profile of Jesus Christ and in turn show the true glory of His Church. We seek to encourage a deeper appreciation of who Jesus is and to somehow bridge the gap between the first century view of Him and the twenty first century!

Thankfully, accompanying this desire, there is a spiritual power and supernatural dynamic; Jesus is walking amongst the Church! Together with the Holy Spirit, we are creatively working to see our world impacted with an irresistible Christ portrayed with increasing power and appealing irresistibility.

The Church
God loves the Church. Jesus is building His Church; but the Church can no longer be a place of political intrigue or sedition. The Church can no longer be a place of schisms and splits based upon personal preferences. It can no longer be a place of self-indulgent memories. The Church must stop its pretentions and petty grandstanding; no one's looking!

The Church has to stop the revolving door syndrome where if you get upset or offended one Sunday, you just go to the church down the street. The Church must stop the supermarket syndrome of special prices and out of the ordinary offers. We have to counter the consumer mentality in the Church. Church is NOT a McDonald's "drive thru"!

We've gotten carried away doing things the Church was never meant to do and placing our emphasis on things that are secondary to our message and mission. So many times we as church leaders we get carried away by "noble distractions."

We've lost our passion to communicate Christ to a world who doesn't know Him, preferring to be self-absorbed and self-indulgent in our religion. We've become experts on teaching people how to have a great marriage, better sex and a balanced budget but we've neglected to point them towards Jesus Christ and salvation. I know this sounds tough, and to some it may sound harsh, but it is true.

While the world goes to Hell we just want to feel "close to Jesus", have an open microphone down the front of church to give our prophecy and sing our own special songs to Jesus. We indulge ourselves while the world around us suffers from the effects of sin and we just want to make sure the music isn't too loud please – I want to be able to hear my own voice. Oh! And can we please have some more "meat of the word" please?

While people live in darkness in a hostile and fallen world, the Church is arguing with each other over stuff they shouldn't and getting offended over stuff they should find the grace to work through.

The time has come for a Church to arise now with grace and power to re-present the King of an everlasting Kingdom and His culture upon this sin soaked Earth. To preach Jesus Christ and Him crucified in the power of the Spirit; to show the thousands upon thousands of the personal aspects of Jesus to a world in such great need of a Saviour and Redeemer. To portray Him as not only a God but as a man who loves and relates to us.

Context is Vital to Understand

As we look at the first century spread of the gospel, Corinth or even Rome is a better context for us than Jerusalem. If we were to simply study the context of the Jerusalem Church's expansion, we would not fully understand or comprehend the power of the gospel as it affected people from outside the Jewish faith.

It was men like Paul and the twelve disciples of Jesus who took the good news to every place in Asia Minor and Western Europe, including Corinth and Rome. Paul understood the Prophet Isaiah when he said in **Acts 13:47**, "For this is what the Lord has commanded us: "'I have made you a light for the Gentiles, that you may bring salvation to the ends of the Earth.'"

Corinth was, to all intents and purposes, the sex capital of Asia Minor. It was a place of pagan rituals and notorious immorality. The worship of Venus, whose temple was on the top of the Acrocorinthus, was attended with shameless decadence where thousands of female slaves were maintained for the service of worshippers.

In Paul's day, it was the capital city of Achaia, a region and city re-founded by Julius Caesar and had become a centre also for Greek philosophers. It was a place where many Jews had fled during the reign of Roman Emperor Claudius and hence Paul's initial outreach was to them. But soon his ministry went beyond just the Jewish community and he broke out into the other non-Jewish communities speaking with great boldness and the Lord was with him.

Much like Europe today, Corinth and Rome posed a great challenge to Paul and his team as they sought to preach the good news of Jesus there. The similarities to our society today are striking yet encouraging because Paul and his team were successful in planting large and significant churches there. I think in this current climate in the West, we too can see the impact of the Church as never before!

Corinth and Rome were pre-Christian; let me explain. In these cities of Asia Minor and Europe there was no understanding of Jesus there. Most people in the city had no knowledge of the scriptures, most had never heard of Jesus Christ, most had never seen a Biblical scroll, and most had never known there was the possibility to have a relationship with the God who created it all.

In the truest sense of the word, the people of Corinth and Rome were **ignorant** of Christ and His claims. Much like Europe has become today, Corinth and cities like Rome were hot beds of darkness and sin. Paul and his band of preachers had a huge task before them.

Their context in Corinth was that of a pantheon of religions. There was no sense of what we would call a "Judeo-Christian ethic" to life. It was correct to say they had low morals; in fact it was even more correct to say they had NO MORALS.

Their values were not based upon the God who created the world but upon many deities and lesser gods who fought and argued with each other. Their world was an erotic world where there was no law or concept of fidelity, monogamy or code of sexual conduct. Their pictures of God were damaged and corrupted by their lifestyle and world views.

Content
Though the context of the first century and the twenty first century are staggering and complex, it should never affect our content; though it will have bearing on our style and communication; our message must retain its purity. Through the agency of common grace we can give a Biblical explanation of who Jesus is. The word of God is the great reveal of Christ by the power of the Holy Spirit.

Let's make sure that we never compromise the message. Let's be sure we are seeking to communicate all that God desired us to communicate and to do so in the dynamic of a relationship with the Holy Spirit.

I have a premise I work from; I believe we must do all we can do so that God is free to do what only God can do. I can't save a soul, that's God job. However, I can create an atmosphere that is culturally relevant so someone can come in and easily connect to the message of Christ.

Remember Christ is both divine and human; He is God and He is Man. Our approach to modern communications must always allow for both human communications (all we can do) and divine communication (the stuff that only God can do).

Paul said in **1 Corinthians 2** that he "did not come with eloquence or superior wisdom" His resolve was to know nothing except "Jesus Christ and Him crucified". It was not a matter of accident, or chance, that Paul made Christ his great and constant theme, but it was his deliberate purpose and it should be ours too.

His determination was to preach Jesus Christ. He determined the message would be about the deity and divine nature of Christ and to preach His crucifixion, His earthly role in providing our salvation. If Jesus had not been both God *and* Man, He would never have been able to deliver such a great salvation.

Paul knew the Greek world had a penchant for philosophies, intellectual debates and the subtleties of language with its flourishes and its graceful and finished elocution. His determination was to not fall for their Gnostic beliefs and existential explanations. His strategy was to cut through the bull and make the message clear. His determination was to make sure the message was based around one grand theme; his resolve was to know nothing amongst them but "...Jesus Christ and Him crucified"!

However, the message he sought to communicate relied upon a God of miracles, a God of power and substance. The message at its core was a supernatural message. This is why he said he had come to them "in weakness and fear, and with much trembling."

He didn't come in the showiness of his brilliant personality nor did he flaunt his educational credentials. The message he communicated was a miraculous message about a God of love who had prepared the world for the arrival of His Son to show us what He was like.

Plain View

A trap for the modern Church to avoid is not to spend all our time giving out DIY sermons. Let's not fill our sermon schedules with only "how to live better" sermons. This generation is profoundly theologically ignorant and it has become debilitating to say the least. But let's never forsake the power of theology communicated in a modern and contemporary style. Let us never stop making Jesus famous by continuing to declare His nature, character and gospel.

This same Christ who became the ultimate sacrifice for the sins of the entire world also rose again defeating sin and death. A message that would have been seen as madness to many and if not for the power of the Holy Spirit to bring revelation, he was doomed in his mission and his message would have been laughed out of the arena!

In a world familiar with religions, cults, gods and goddesses, blood sacrifices, atonement and redemptions, Paul knew His message would relate to this crowd, his audience. The imagery of blood was understandable to most in the ancient world. The ability to communicate that the Christ (or Messiah) who had come to die for the sins of all mankind had arrived, depended on the work of the Holy Spirit and the word of God being preached.

The message required, even demanded, the authority of the One who had commissioned it. Paul knew and understood the power of this. The message of Christ is not only supernatural and miraculous at the core but also timeless and unchanging. He believed that if you would dare to believe it you would connect to the power source that created the heavens and the Earth. This message will bring with it a salvation that can only be explained by a risen Christ and the awesome authority of the God's Holy Spirit.

The act of salvation is a supernatural action of God. I can't save anyone – this is an act of God – it is powerful, supernatural and absolutely miraculous! Remember this; the Church is not primarily about worship styles, or ministries, or gifts. The Church is not primarily about being cool, or having the latest fashions. At the heart of all we do is the desire to proclaim a message about Jesus Christ that leads to a transformation of the heart of mankind!

Our churches are seeking to reflect a first century Jesus alongside of His desire to build a twenty first century Church with an authentic message of salvation and the power of a new life.

Noble Distractions

Jesus was driven by a mission and His Church is to reflect this. However, many churches today seem to have got this part a bit wrong. Some churches are music driven, others are miracle driven and others still are ministry driven, while some are driven by a special message like faith or maybe prosperity.

Some are driven by the needs of the poor but hardly ever speak about a relationship with the risen Christ. Some are driven by the need to relieve human suffering but never get the chance to share the message of salvation.

The first century Church of the New Testament was all about Jesus, His mission and His message. He was the core personality, the prime mover and the absolute super star. The first century Church, as it moved out from its base of Jerusalem, hardly ever spoke about the God of Israel but sought to introduce the audience to Jesus Christ and through Him then go on to explain who God was. They were fanatical about being a witness of Jesus Christ and they were accompanied by the fire and power of the Holy Spirit.

The twenty first century Church needs to reflect this paradigm and to do so powerfully. There can be no place for a man driven Church where we serve personalities and make them our super stars. No more putting people on a pedestal. In the last few years we've seen too many of them fall from the heights. There is room for only one superstar and His name is Jesus!

The content of the first century Church was a message about Jesus; his death and resurrection, His salvation and His grace. The first

Plain View

century Church had one message and it was to lift up Jesus Christ by the power of the Holy Spirit, declaring the good news and giving people room to receive the message.

They had no problems when it came to discipleship either. They were not distracted in the distinction between evangelism and discipleship. They understood the dynamic of what Jesus said when he commanded them to "go AND make disciples"[123]. For many, evangelism and discipleship are separate agenda items. In the minds of many church leaders they appear separate and distinct; not so for the first century Church. We think in terms of either winning people to Christ or trying to establish people in Christ.

I think the words of Jesus are sheer genius when in **Matthew 28:19** He says, "Therefore go and make disciples ..." Evangelism and discipleship are part of the "great commission." It's a both/and not an either/or. Jesus is saying that as you engage in witness, you are being discipled. Evangelism is discipleship. Jesus did not say go and then make disciples, He said go and make disciples and do this hand in hand.

Subtle changes take place within our churches when we distinguish between the two and emphasize discipleship over the other. It is a matter of focus. It is a matter of goals and motivation that translates into the energy that propels a church forward. For some it has become a noble distraction.

In a recent blog post, I mention the fact that Jesus is happy for us to leave the ninety nine sheep and go in search for the lost one. I believe that shepherding the sheep is vital but I think in the scheme of things in church life we "over-pastor" our people and give them little chance to grow themselves.

---

[123] Matthew 28:19

It is troubling when we try and put on offer things in the Church that were meant to be accessed through our relationship with God. It is impossible to sustain a Church culture that tries to continually meet people's needs when the needs we seek to meet were to be met by Christ in God. Subtly, our emphasis shifts from Jesus to the Church.

Psalms 46:1 says that *"**God is our refuge and strength**, an ever-present help in trouble."* We must never promote the Church as a sanctuary that replaces God as our refuge. Subtle shifts take place within a church's impact when we substitute Church for Christ.

God desires a relationship with us and we need to encourage His people to directly access Him through His word. We need to trust the Holy Spirit is working within people and that they are being renewed as they offer themselves to Him in spiritual devotion.

I know it sounds scary to those who love to "over pastor" God's people. I know it sounds almost heartless to those who feel they need a pastor to look after them instead of learning to stand on their own two feet before God. Yes, we need to do everything we can to bless people and help people mature and grow but there are some things that only God can do. Having maturity in God helps you to make that distinction.

This is one reason why some people become disillusioned with church life. It's because we are teaching people to bypass God and come to the Church instead. It is a subtle detour and short circuits true discipleship. It's hard to wean people off the Church and get them to go to God instead. Maturity is being able to distinguish when to go to God and when to receive from others.

The modern challenge is how can we be more like Jesus if we don't know who He really is today? Or how we co-labour with Christ in building the Church of His dreams if we don't know what the Church was really meant to be? How do we become an accurate representation of Christ and His Church if we don't know what it was He sought to represent?

How do we re-present Jesus to the twenty first century with all of His power, mystery and passion? How do we explain to a scientific and online world the supernatural nature of Jesus; a Jesus of miracles, of signs and wonders? How do we re-present Christ to a world on a spiritual journey and have no accurate images of Jesus? How to we describe the transforming power of a relationship with Jesus when the world today has turned their back on Jesus?

How do we present a Jesus rich in grace, abounding in mercy and abundant with favour towards you? This is a true picture of Jesus! He is ancient, timeless, eternal and utterly in love with you. He is interested in every facet of who you are, your daily life, your trials and tribulations, your joys and your discoveries, your loves and your hurts. Jesus is fascinated with who you are, your destiny and future!

Earthly princes and presidents look greatest at a distance, surrounded with pomp; but Jesus needs no earthly status. The more closely He is viewed, the more He stands in peerless majesty and dignity. The closer you examine Him, the more you'll see the flawlessness of His divinity, the splendour of his humanity. He rested His teaching on His own authority, and the claim was felt by all.

Our challenge is to present a first century Christ for a twenty first century Church; powerful and strong, bold and ancient; able to deliver. This is Jesus who is aware of our destiny and desires to work with us to achieve greatness in this life and the one to follow. This is Jesus who is able to forgive us our sins, wash us clean and keep us clean. This is Jesus who is able to make us stand in His grace and walk under His favour!

This is Jesus; strong, robust, unafraid of demons and spirits, powerful in the face of opposition. He is solid, durable and tough; no one can stand against Him. Even the weakest saint upon his knee will make the powers of darkness shudder and shake with fear.

This is Jesus - Son of God - who, when he died for the sins of the world, confronted not only the Devil but our last enemy; Death. Jesus took back the sceptre of life and the keys of death and Hell and defeated them both as he was raised to new life by the Holy Spirit. Not even death could hold Him; this is a Christ who is mighty to save.

It is this Jesus who said in **Matthew 16:18**, "I will build my Church, and the gates of Hades will not overcome it." It will be a Church expansive with energy, passionate, vibrant, creative, innovative and original, a fresh and relevant Church, and a twenty first century Church for today!

Plain View

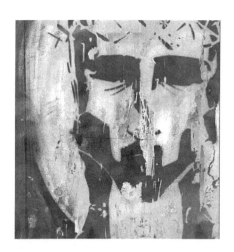

Jesus Christ: Radical beyond measure

Part Four: Never Before Seen Footage of Jesus Christ

No one can read the gospels without feeling the actual presence of Jesus. His personality pulsates in every word. No myth is filled with such life. **Albert Einstein.**

The true work of art is but a shadow of the divine perfection. **Michelangelo.**

Jesus Christ, Jesus Christ, Who are you? What have you sacrificed? Jesus Christ Superstar, Do you think you're what they say you are? **Rice & Webber**, Chorus of Jesus Christ Superstar.

Chapter 10: Living in the Question

Nicole Conner[124] – via Facebook – December 2010: "Living in the question, the contradictions, and the many non-defined boundaries is so very difficult for us; we want answers, neat boxes, true dogma, security and certainty. Our desire for the latter is maybe what causes us to exchange the wild and unnerving walk of faith for ice cold behaviour modification or religion."

Jim Johnson:[125] "We believe that in the expressions of our culture—music, film, books, TV—we can hear the heart cry of people asking the deep questions of life. When we acknowledge these sentiments and let them be heard in our weekend services, we create connection points with seekers that enable us then to speak God's words of truth into their lives."

I regularly get the question: "How do you use the theology of common grace to lead people to special grace?" These next few chapters are my attempt to show how I do it. As a team, we've taken a risk by doing these kinds of messages and I can with a good confidence say that we pulled it off more times than not. People started to get it and started to use the system to start a conversation

---

[124] http://www.markconner.com.au
[125] Jim Johnson is a co-founding and senior pastor of Preston Trail Community Church, Frisco, Texas

with their unchurched friends; it started to work. So enjoy the practical examples of what we did. Please remember, I'm not prescribing that you do them without laying the good foundations that took us a number of years to lay.

Jesus Christ Superstar....

Jesus Christ Superstar was a rock opera that commenced on Broadway in 1971 – it was a creation of Tim Rice and Andrew Lloyd Webber. It was a Broadway hit and was incredibly popular – the theme song is still recognized by most generations today.

The rock opera has been playing regularly around the world and did a four year stint in the UK from 2000 – 2004 and was staged in Spain and in South Korea earlier in 2012. It is a revival musical and still incredibly popular today including in Bratislava, Slovakia!

Rice and Webber sought to bring the story of Jesus to the big stage, and the rock opera went on to become a movie as well. The story is about the last week of Jesus' life before the crucifixion and the resurrection. According to *Wikipedia*, *Jesus Christ Superstar* "highlights the political and interpersonal struggles of Judas Iscariot with Jesus and his claims to be God."

The musical follows the Bible's accounts of the last weeks of Jesus' life, beginning with Jesus and his followers arriving in Jerusalem and ending with the crucifixion. What captured the mind and the attention of the day was Rice and Webber's uses of twentieth century attitudes and sensibilities as well as the use of contemporary slang (which pervaded the lyrics) and the allusions to modern life which are scattered throughout the political depiction of the events.

A large part of the plot focuses on the character of Judas who is depicted as a conflicted, tragic figure who is not satisfied with what he views as Jesus' lack of planning, and he becomes alarmed by Jesus' claims of divinity.

Plain View

Remarkably, the Church during the early 70s was in shock over the rock opera and complained bitterly of seeing Jesus clad with jeans. It disturbed the Church of the day because it seemed to accommodate the views of Judas Iscariot instead of focus on the claims of Christ's divinity. The Church were upset by the contemporary way in which Rice and Webber brought Jesus back to main stay culture. The Church went on the attack, criticising the producers.

For Rice and Webber, their Jesus was not enshrined in a church, over spiritualized, dogmatized and rationalized. For Rice and Webber, He was a folk hero ready for the big stage of Broadway! He was vital, youthful, enthusiastic, good looking and smiled a lot. Oh and did I mention, He wore jeans and had long hair!

Their Jesus was portrayed as someone *in their world* as the kind of hero who is rejected and crucified in the same ways that youth with their ideas and ideals were often rejected and crucified by society.

As you watch the rock opera on stage or listen to the sound track you get a strong feeling of identification, on the part of Rice and Webber, with Jesus. One quote from a Broadway review reads like this; "Webber and Rice have made an important, if not altogether artistically satisfying, contribution to our culture. Their work seems far more honest, theologically, than many "Christian" musicals and reviews written by and for "Christians.""

They depicted a Jesus who was a folk-hero of the youth culture of the day. Their work was a musical that asks, again honestly, questions about who is Jesus Christ. Perhaps their Christology is best stated in their own words, in which Jesus is asked to defend his claim to divinity:

"Jesus Christ Superstar, do you think you're what they say you are? . . . Who d'you think besides yourself's the pick of the crop? Buddha, was he where it's at? Is he where you are? Could Mohammed move a mountain or was that just PR?" Jesus Christ, Jesus Christ – who are you . . . ?

The Religious View...

In The Message, **Matthew 10-11** says this: "Later when Jesus was eating supper at Matthew's house with his close followers, a lot of disreputable characters came and joined them. When the Pharisees saw him keeping this kind of company, they had a fit, and lit into Jesus' followers. "What kind of example is this from your Teacher, acting cosy with crooks and riffraff?" Jesus, overhearing, shot back, "Who needs a doctor: the healthy or the sick? Go figure out what this Scripture means: 'I'm after mercy, not religion.' I'm here to invite outsiders, not coddle insiders."

With this scripture ringing in my ears, I suppose what annoys me the most is the attitudes of the Church! The religious not only had a view, but made it public. They saw the musical as a threat instead of the awesome opportunity it presented. The Church of the day, much like today's Church, continues to define itself by what it opposes instead of identifying with the abundant life promised by Jesus. They condemned the musical outright! They judged it unfit for Christian consumption.

The Church continues to be negative, legalistic and against stuff instead of demonstrating the grace and favour of God on a culture and society ignorant of the true claims of Jesus Christ. It appears to me that some in the Church can't see the signs of Christ in pop culture today and continue to miss incredible opportunities to make comment and engage with people.

Instead of applauding the efforts of Rice and Webber and using this play as an opportunity to tell others about a Christ who was cool and hip and now, thanks to the efforts of these two young producers, a folk hero. Instead they reverted to the old paradigm of the Church hiding behind its four walls, criticising and being threatened because this Jesus wore jeans!

Plain View

Instead of seeing the fact that the Holy Spirit had once again gone before the Church of the day to prepare a platform for the Church to engage with pop culture the Church reacted, closed ranks and was negative.

Instead of recognising the resonance of Christ in popular culture, the Church disengaged with culture and society again to be something the Church was not meant to be. Jesus called the Church to be light, we were not called to kick the darkness; we were called to shine.

The role of the Church is secured by the power of God and by the Church continuing to engage with today. We are the light to the world showing a way to connect with God, Christ and His Church. We continue to see resonance and see the signs that Christ has gone before us to prepare the hearts and minds of people around us to receive this powerful message.

We will continue to cosy up with crooks and riff raff, recognising these people as our audience. We will continue to engage with people in our world today because it's them who need a revelation of who Jesus is and why He came to Earth, died and was raised again to new life. Jesus said He was here to invite outsiders not to coddle insiders! I love this translation! I want to invite outsiders too! I get annoyed by spending too much time "coddling insiders!" I love hanging out with riff raff!

What I loved about the rock opera *Jesus Christ Superstar* was it brought Jesus out of the closet of organised religion and onto the stage of Broadway. Rice and Webber were, I believe, used by God to make Jesus famous once again.

These two guys were used by God to introduce Jesus Christ to another generation. Common grace takes a bow again! One reviewer of the movie commented that Jesus looked hot! How this contrasted with the Church's picture of Christ as a stark, pale, painfully thin and agonised person.

Rice and Webber portrayed a Jesus full of life, vigour and passion. He was portrayed to a new generation as a hero, as someone who could sympathise with the feelings of a generation and was relevant. He laughed, broke into song and was good-looking. He also showed authentic feelings and understood rejection, misunderstanding and betrayal from friends. He was a real live person. I believe this is a true picture of Jesus. Jesus was an incredibly attractive person, people loved being around Him and enjoyed His messages and His stories.

This is the continuing challenge of the Church; to re-present Jesus Christ to our "today"!

The scriptures say this about Him in **Matthew 7:28-29**: "When Jesus had finished saying these things, the crowds were amazed at his teaching, because he taught as one who had authority, and not as their teachers of the law." People love Jesus; if only they could get the chance to SEE him and TOUCH Him.

In **John 7:46**, people described Jesus' messages like this; "No-one ever spoke the way this man does." He was loved by the crowd; he amazed them with miraculous powers from God and stunned them with His practical but heavenly teaching. They loved Him as a person and they loved Him for the way He dealt with others. He showed compassion, mercy and grace. He never condemned any one and actually added dignity to the lowliest of them all.

They loved His miracles. They loved the fact that where ever He went there was a sense of anticipation that miracles would happen. Jesus was guaranteed to intervene into their lives, that, as God in the flesh, He had the ability to intrude into their world and existence.
After His resurrection and ascension back to Heaven and after the giving of the Holy Spirit signifying the birth of the New Testament Church, the basis for all the miraculous was the salvation of a soul. The greatest miracle ever will always be the salvation of an individual or family. Salvation – regeneration – the forgiveness of sin and the reconnection with God and eternity remain the firm foundation of all

miracles. Flowing out of that great intervention of God into our lives is the benefit of knowing a miracle working God. Out of the gospel flows the power of God to do the impossible and make the impossible, possible. We have an all-powerful God who continues to intervene in our lives.

I suppose what really challenges me about the musical *Jesus Christ Superstar* is that Rice and Webber did exactly what the Church should have been doing from the beginning. They brought Jesus to the forefront of modern society and popular culture. They put Jesus on Broadway! They brought Him to the big screen! They made Him famous for another generation!

Rice and Webber asked and answered the question of who is Jesus; He is a superstar! He is a superstar supported by a great cast of supporting actors and actresses, His Church! Is it any wonder at His birth the Magi were guided to the stables in Bethlehem by a great star!

This whole concept challenges me as the lead pastor of my own church. I'm tired of Jesus being the best kept secret here in our city and beyond. I don't want Jesus and His awesome power to connect this generation with God and eternity to be a secret any more. Why can't the Church be as attractive as Jesus Christ?

I like the Message translation where it says in **Matthew 5: 14-16** "Here's another way to put it: You're here to be light, bringing out the God-colours in the world. God is not a secret to be kept. We're going public with this, as public as a city on a hill. If I make you light-bearers, you don't think I'm going to hide you under a bucket, do you? I'm putting you on a light stand. Now that I've put you there on a hilltop, on a light stand—shine! Keep open house; be generous with your lives. By opening up to others, you'll prompt people to open up with God, this generous Father in heaven."

We might not be able to afford the lavish production costs of presenting a rock opera like *Jesus Christ Superstar* and we may never be front page news with our local paper, but **each one of us can make Jesus famous in our world**. Our priority is to go into our world and seek out the signs that Christ has gone before us and then, by the Holy Spirit's power, be helpful to others in their journey to find Jesus Christ. We rely implicitly on the Holy Spirit to go before us and prepare the hearts of others for our message.

Who is Jesus?

When I "Googled" the phrase "Who is Jesus" - it returned an amazing 596,000 web pages. Without the quotation marks it returned an awesome 45 million pages. From Google stats, this is obviously an oft asked question by many. My prayer is that our twenty first century Church will take seriously the responsibility to present Jesus to our world in a way they can grasp and understand who He is.

There is no doubt that Jesus Christ is one of the most fascinating figures in history. He is one of the most controversial, intriguing and maybe even spellbinding of all historical figures.

H.G. Wells, an English science fiction writer, said "I am an historian, I am not a believer, but I must confess as a historian that this penniless preacher from Nazareth is irrevocably the very centre of history. Jesus Christ is easily the most dominant figure in all history."

Who is Jesus? In the words of H.G. Wells he is "the most dominate figure in all history."

Kenneth Scott LaTourette, an American historian and academic of great note, said "As the centuries pass, the evidence is accumulating that, measured by His effect on history, Jesus is the most influential life ever lived on this planet."

Who is Jesus Christ? In the words of Kenneth Scott LaTourette He is "the most influential life ever lived on this planet."

Albert Einstein, an iconic figure of the twentieth century - a German born theoretical physicist, once said: "As a child I received instruction both in the Bible and in the Talmud. I am a Jew, but I am enthralled by the luminous figure of the Nazarene....No one can read the gospels without feeling the actual presence of Jesus. His personality pulsates in every word."

Who is Jesus? In the words of Albert Einstein, a "luminous figure ... His personality pulsates in every word."

Let me quote from an unusual source; **Pete Larson.** Pete Larson is another icon, one most of you would never have heard of. He is an American palaeontologist and currently the President of Black Hills Institute of Geological Research Inc. and author of two books. His first book was entitled *Sexual Dimorphism in the Abundant Upper Cretaceous Theropod, T. Rex.* His second a runaway best seller called *Rex Appeal* and it followed on from the first.

He said; "Despite our efforts to keep him out, God intrudes. The life of Jesus is bracketed by two impossibilities: 'a virgin's womb and an empty tomb'. Jesus entered our world through a door marked, 'No Entrance' and left through a door marked "No Exit."

Who is Jesus Christ? In the words of Pete Larson; He is God's intrusion!

Talk about a dramatic entrance and exit! Ladies and gentlemen, it was indeed a show stopper!

The counter to cynicism, the proof of our genuineness, is simply this: our longing for something better; our longing for higher purpose and meaning, a higher moral consciousness of our own making that rises far above their expectations. Cynics have no riposte to this. We know first-hand our longings to be true. **Joseph D. Jacques, *Chivalry-Now: The Code of Male Ethics***

Chapter 11: *Avatar* – Longing for Something Better

No one who's seen this film will deny that it is cinematography at its best! Many people believe *Avatar* had redefined the medium of cinema. The movie is awesome, fantastic and mind blowing. The colour, the characters, the plot (though some would say a bit tired and predictable) the animals and the 3D, it was all simply phenomenal!

The film is a visual wonder. One sequence when Jake learns to fly a Pandoran dragon through the planet's floating islands is, alone, worth the price of admission. The grace and beauty of that scene literally brought tears to my eyes.

No one can doubt Cameron's artistic genius when it comes to bringing to the screen this fantastical, mythical world. It represents the best expression of what J.R.R. Tolkien meant when he said that we are to be "sub-creators" with the Creator. Cameron's vision is so powerfully and beautifully rendered that it's easy to imagine a world like Pandora actually existing.

Perhaps the great success of James Cameron's film *Avatar* is that he unwittingly emphasizes our need for God and relationship with Him. Let me explain. A recent article on CNN's Entertainment website highlights an unexpected phenomenon associated with the movie *Avatar*: Fans who long for the alien world Pandora, feel depressed and suicidal because it's unattainable.

We're not talking about a few teenagers in despair, but tens of thousands of people from all ages filled with despair, desolation, anguish and hopelessness. They are so hooked on hopelessness they wrote on the site forum to express their misery! According to fans of the film, compared with life on Earth, Pandora is a beautiful, glowing utopia.

The problem is that is Pandora's an entirely fictional place. It's not just out of reach, its non-existent! So why are so many people so obsessed with it?

Fans commenting on an online forum say Pandora seems to be a perfect place, a pristine world where there is synergy between all of the characters. In their words, it's a world with "something we don't have here on Earth."

But we did have a pristine world once. There was a place where man and God walked together in perfect harmony. It was beautiful, awesome and beyond our explanation. Then man sinned; he disobeyed God and as a result, we don't live harmoniously, and won't, until Christ comes again. Sin came into our human existence, like a virus it infected every person ever born to flesh and blood.

Created in God's Image
According to the creation account in Genesis, God created man "...in our image, in our likeness." God Himself is an eternal being with no beginning or end. He has perfect knowledge and perfect understanding, and God is love. Created in His image, we carry certain aspects of His divine nature. Like Him, we have "eternity in our hearts"[126] and eventually we will dwell with Him.

Ecclesiastes 3:11 in the Amplified Bibles says, "He has made everything beautiful in its time. He also has planted eternity in men's hearts and minds [a divinely implanted sense of a purpose working through the ages which nothing under the sun but God alone can

---

[126] Ecclesiastes 3:11

satisfy], yet so that men cannot find out what God has done from the beginning to the end.

This eternity placed inside our hearts is "a divine sense of purpose". It is a sense of purpose that God created and only God can fill.

In the book of Revelation, the Apostle John described the new heaven and new Earth as the dwelling place of God, where He will live with man. "He will wipe every tear from their eyes. There will be no more death or mourning or crying or pain, for the old order of things has passed away." **Revelation 21:4**

This 'new heaven and new Earth' is a hope for all who believe in Christ. Eternal life is a promise given to each individual who turns from unbelief to faith in Christ. It is a changing of our mind about God and when we do make this change and decide to believe, we inherit life eternal and an a open loving relationship with God who stands with open arms wanting desperately to embrace each of us as His child. A relationship with a loving God, a promise of life (and "life more abundant"[127]) as well as the promise of life eternal are all great hopes of the believer's life.

Longing for Something Better

Doesn't that sound like what the fans of *Avatar* are longing for? Aren't we all longing for something better, something perfect, and something that seems unobtainable?

Yet U2's song, *I Still Haven't Found What I'm Looking For*, resonated in the hearts of multiplied millions of people all over the world. The reason is we are searching by nature, within each of us is the desire for beauty, perfection and love. People want direction, guidance, peace and satisfaction. People are looking for hope. Yet in the words of a 20th century poet and prophet Mick Jagger, most are saying, "I can't get no satisfaction."

---

[127] John 10:10

C. S. Lewis once said, "If I have a desire which no experience in this world can satisfy, the explanation is I was made for another world." Cameron's movie rightly depicts Earth as a dying planet, but his promise of a utopia on another planet is an empty one. The writer of Proverbs would call that "a hope deferred," which "makes the heart sick." **(Proverbs 13:12)**

The unrelenting assertion by those who insist there is no God only magnifies the futility of hoping for anything better. If this world is all there is to life, then seeing something as promising as Pandora would lead to depression, and perhaps even suicidal thoughts.

But There's More to This Life
But the good news is that there's more to this life than the world around us. There IS a God and He intervenes regularly in human affairs. God didn't create us to find satisfaction in His creation, but in Him. God is the object of our searching; God is the fulfilment of our seeking. Some people describe the longing we feel as a "God-shaped hole," which only He can fill.

But what does man do? He ignores this hole, or attempts to fill it with things other than God: imaginary worlds, business, family, materialism, sports, and accomplishments. That's why life is never satisfactory. We look to other things and other people – anywhere but to God.

Where Is Hope?
Is there hope for those who are so sadly affected by *Avatar*? There is, but it won't be found on message boards, in playing video games, or watching the movie countless times. Nothing created by any human being will bring the satisfaction we crave. It will only be found in relationship with Jesus Christ. He alone satisfies and fills the emptiness of our lives.

Hope

The Biblical word "hope" means "a confident expectation of good." **Hebrews 11:1** says that hope is a vital ingredient to faith in that "... faith is being sure of what we hope for and certain of what we do not see."

Now we need to take great care here in our understanding of faith and hope. Our faith is in God, in God's word and consequently in His nature and character. There are times when pandemonium runs amok and we're in the middle of uproar, trials and hard times. This is not the time to pull away but the exercise hope and faith in God and His unchanging nature.

"He gives strength to the weary and increases the power of the weak. Even youths grow tired and weary, and young men stumble and fall; but those who hope in the LORD will renew their strength. They will soar on wings like eagles; they will run and not grow weary, they will walk and not be faint." **Isaiah 40:29-31**

Our hope is in God.

Tom Rawls

I am an historian, I am not a believer, but I must confess as a historian that this penniless preacher from Nazareth is irrevocably the very centre of history. Jesus Christ is easily the most dominant figure in all history. **H.G. Wells**, British author.

The truth is incontrovertible. Malice may attack it, ignorance may deride it, but in the end, there it is. **Winston Churchill.**

Chapter 12: *Angels & Demons* – The Hunt for Truth

"All truths are easy to understand once they are discovered; the point is to discover them."
Galileo

This movie is all about uncovering the **truth**; searching for truth, uncovering the lie and finding out what is true!

The truth is important; the human heart cries out for it.

King Solomon, the wisest man in the world, once said "It is the glory of God to conceal a matter; to search out a matter is the glory of kings." **Proverbs 25:2**

The hunger for truth is intrinsic to our human hearts; so to tell a lie violates our heart and conscience. Telling a lie breaks something on the inside – the more you lie the more irreparable the heart becomes. Telling lies damages others in the process too.

Nadine Gordimer, South African writer and Nobel laureate, once wrote; "The truth isn't always beauty, but the hunger for it is." The hunger for truth is in the heart of every person.

WE WANT TO KNOW THE TRUTH! WE HATE BEING LIED TO!

John Locke, famous English philosopher, once said; "To love truth for truth's sake is the principle part of human perfection in this world, and the seed-plot of all other virtues." What he's saying is it is a human virtue to seek after truth; and it is God's desire to reveal it.

Why do we like to watch those "who-done-it" movies? Have you ever wondered why? Because we want to KNOW! Truth matters, truth is important and truth is imperative; even when we watch a TV show. Truth always triumphs. You know what I mean don't you? Getting to the bottom of a situation is important; we need to know the truth. It is written into our very DNA! We must unravel the truth, we must expose the lie. We're like a dog with a bone!

We've all experienced that conflict of hearing two sides to a story and knowing someone is lying; but who is it? You can feel that tension in the air; truth has a certain ring and lies most of the time just don't ring true. You can sense something is off; you can feel it's not right.

There is an old Chinese proverb; "Three things cannot long be hidden the sun, the moon, and the truth."

That is the problem with lies; they are so easily exposed by the truth.

Abraham Lincoln once said; "You can fool some of the people all of the time, and all of the people some of the time, but you cannot fool all of the people all of the time."

Eventually the truth will come out. Because of the nature of truth, it will triumph.

- We need to know the truth even if it hurts.
- We need to tell the truth even if the truth will hurt.
- Something inside of every one of us needs to expose the lie!

Apart from a clear and disturbing pathology, our heart's desire is for truth; to hear the truth and to tell the truth as well.

Plain View

Angels & Demons is a movie about truth and lies. It is a cracking good story too! It has all the essentials of a great Hollywood film; but it has very little to do with the subject of either angels or demons.

The movie opens with the death of the Pope and is surrounded by the ancient and mysterious ritual practices of the Catholic Church. The backdrop is of course Rome and Vatican City. There are many opulent scenes of both. We see first-hand how the Catholic Church goes about finding a new Pope.

Contrasting with these ancient proceedings is an ultra-modern and high tech facility seeking to produce a new kind of energy that could change the world. The new energy is ironically called "The God Particle".

The tension of the movie is that this God Particle has been stolen and turned into an explosive device and hidden somewhere in Vatican City. This stolen device becomes the centre piece of the movie as four of the cardinals from the Preferinni have been kidnapped and are being murdered. An elaborate conspiracy is being set up. Just how elaborate, no one really knows until the very end of the movie where a shocking twist concludes the movie.

Enter Tom Hanks as symbolist Professor Robert Langdon. He is asked to help investigate the supposed re-emergence of the ancient secret society called the Illuminati. He has to find the bomb and save the cardinal from being murdered. The name Illuminati, interestingly enough, simply means "enlightened".

What does God say about Truth and Lies?

In **John 8:44**, Jesus makes it clear who the Original Liar is in His speech to the religious leaders around Him; "You belong to your father, the devil, and you want to carry out your father's desire. He was a murderer from the beginning, not holding to the truth, for there is no truth in him. When he lies, he speaks his native language, for he is a liar and the father of lies."

When the Devil lies he speaks his native tongue, for he *is* a liar, and notice the designation Jesus gives him: "The father of lies." When we lie – we are speaking the Devil's language.

Have you ever been lied to? When we lie or are lied to it involves deception, dishonesty and fraud. The minute a lie is spoken, there begins a search for the truth. A lie is a comment that is untrue; it is usually spoken to deceive someone; usually to keep a secret. The goal of a lie is deceit or deception.

It is interesting that the words "trust" and "truth" are linked words. Truth carries high value in the Kingdom of God; as lying brings judgement, so truth has it rewards. In **John 8:31-32**, "Jesus said, "... you will know the truth, and the truth will set you free. ""

In man's search for truth, as the heart cries out for truth, our mission is to find truth, absolute and immovable truth; truth I can base my life upon; an absolute truth. Every man's search for truth is ultimately a search for God, the Truth Teller. **Psalms 84:2** says "My soul yearns, even faints, for the courts of the LORD; my heart and my flesh cry out for the living God."

In many respects the movie *Angels and Demons* explores this tension as well. Robert Langdon doesn't come straight out and say it, but he struggles with his beliefs in God and God's plans.

Right at the end of the movie after he saves the Vatican from being blown up he speaks to the new Camerlengo, personal assistant to the Pope. The PA to the Pope rebuffs Langdon's supposed disbelief in God with a humorous and chiding remark. This is amazing for Hollywood!

Plain View

Sir Arthur Conan Doyle's master sleuth, Sherlock Holmes, once said; "When you have eliminated the impossible, whatever remains, however improbable, must be the truth."

John 14:6: "Jesus answered, "I am the way and the truth and the life. No-one comes to the Father except through me." Jesus didn't say He would lead you to the truth, Jesus said He **was** the truth.

A man who was completely innocent offered himself as a sacrifice for the good of others, including his enemies, and became the ransom of the world. It was a perfect act. **Mahatma Gandhi**[128]

Adventure without risk is Disneyland. **Doug Copeland, author.**

But the love of adventure was in my father's blood. **Buffalo Bill.**

Chapter 13: *Star Trek Into Darkness* – The Human Heart's Yearn for Adventure

Captain's log: Star date 12/06/2015: according to the ancient wisdom of Solomon, God has set eternity in the hearts of men; yet they cannot fathom what God has done from beginning to end. Solomon explains that there is a divinely implanted sense of purpose working in the depths of the human spirit – no one can fathom it and only God alone can satisfy it. These are the voyages of the Starship Enterprise.

Star Trek was the creation of Gene Rodenberry and has developed over 4 decades by producers, script writers, directors and special effects artists to become the second most prolific science fiction franchise in history. The producers of *Star Trek* were surprised by their success and no one could have predicted the stellar rise to fame that gave the series its well-deserved cult status.

Some may ask about its relevance to today; I'm reminded of the movie *Star Trek V: The Final Frontier* where they supposedly come across God. Some of you who know the movie will remember it wasn't really God. Kirk sort of worked it out too when the entity called "God" ask to be transported on the Enterprise and Kirk asked the question, "Why would God need a starship?"

---

[128] **Mohandas Karamchand Gandhi** 2 October 1869 – 30 January 1948 was the pre-eminent political and ideological leader of India during the Indian independence movement.

In our efforts to "look a little closer", we see the impact of *Star Trek* on today's culture remains undeniable; even Google, the world's largest search engine, has a search page dedicated to searches in Klingon!

The writers and producers of *Star Trek* created fantastic new worlds and alternative universes with complexity and detail. They took us to the far flung recesses of the galaxies at Einstein-defying warp speeds. There was a fascinating array of characters ranging from James T Kirk to Spock, from Scotty to Dr. McCoy and Ohura to Mr. Sulu!

The TV series is full of strange and incredible alien beings like Klingons and Vulcans. There was corny dialogue, cheesy humour and there were exotic planets with sets ranging from papier-mâché rocks to the spectacular special effects in the latest movies; did I mention the corny dialogue and weird costumes?! For 40 years now, their mandate has remained the same: "to boldly go where no man has gone before!"

Taking a closer look at this cult TV show allows us the opportunity to see where God has gone ahead, dropping hints of His presence. As we look closer at TV shows like *Star Trek*, we can see the forensic evidence of God's presence, even the ridges of His finger prints become clear for those who dare to take a closer look.

In my review of the show, I see, in general, compelling evidence of Christian resonance. In episodes after episode I see the characters willing to act sacrificially to save the others; I see salvation, redemption and the never ending fight of good against evil. The characters show intense loyalty, gripping friendship and a sense of belonging no matter what quadrant of the universe they happen to be in. It's a friendship we'd love to experience. It makes us long for loyal friends like the cast of the *Star Trek*.

More specifically with the characters: they discover love, wisdom and affirmation; there is significance and intention. It's actually amazing to see a sense of mercy, justice, tolerance and prudence with hope. There is faith with commitment and always a sense of non-judgement with hospitality.

Remarkably, **Karl Rahner,** from his book *Virtual Faith*, is quoted to have said, "The very commonness of everyday things harbour the eternal marvel and silent mystery of God." This eternal marvel and silent mystery is ours to discover!

FOR MEN ONLY! Adventure is bound up in a Man's Heart
I remember when I was 8 years old. My Grandpa had a lake house and, as a family, we would go up to "The Lake" during the holiday times. One Thanksgiving, me and my cousin Jeff were on the pier with my Grandpa and our fathers. It was a manly moment for us; all the guys together.

I made the comment that the water looked dark and a bit spooky. Grandpa turned to Jeff and me and said, "I'll give you each a dollar if you'll jump in and swim to the shore!" I looked at my dad, Jeff turned to his dad; no encouragement either way. I said to Jeff, "I bet I beat you to the shore!" At which point I dove into the murky depths and swam for my life with Jeff seconds behind me! My mother screamed. I could hear her under water. Aunt Janet, Jeff's mother went berserk. The women ran towards the edge of the lake and were frightened for our lives.

That afternoon, Jeff and I were spending our $1 at a local shop, still laughing at the girly way our mothers reacted! We were back slapping and loved the look our Grandpa gave us and the manly way he treated us after that day!

For me, the overwhelming evidence of God behind the script of *Star Trek* is that the show has as its main theme the search for "the final frontier, to explore strange new worlds to seek out new life – to boldly go where no man has gone before."

I love it; "To boldly go where no man has gone before!" The emphasis is to search, seek, explore and to do so with a sense of boldness, courage and daring. It's all about the adventure. It's a spiritual yearning! It's a hunt; a search for fulfilment. This search in our hearts is actually a "hunt" within the hearts of men. This hunt is the siren's call of God; He says, "Come and find me."

As the Church, we identify this search as one of the most profound, provocative, and exciting expressions of legitimate spiritual yearning in at least 100 years.

I am finding that a lot of people are in search of God and God rewards those who earnestly and desperately search for Him. Sometimes in our search we find things masquerading as a God, we chalk it down to experience and move on. Because man is never satisfied until he is filled with what he was created to be filled with, we search until we discover God or die looking.

For so many guys this is the final frontier; this is our journey, this is our challenge to boldly go where we've never been before. We simply cannot settle for the status quo, for the mundane and repetitive living. Within each of us is a desire to rise up against mediocrity and the commonness of life and begin to really live.

To Boldly Go Where No Man Has Gone Before
This phrase, along with its famous split infinitives, resonates with danger and risk. It encourages us to take up the challenge of living, to explore the exhilaration of living life walking the road of risk and doing it boldly.

Mark Twain once said, "Twenty years from now you will be more disappointed by the things that you didn't do than by the ones you did do. So throw off the bowlines. Sail away from the safe harbour. Catch the trade winds in your sails. Explore. Dream. Discover."

It's hard to live life without taking risks. We are confronted by the hard, the difficult and the different and we are challenged by the impossible, the implausible and the unattainable. If we are staggered by them, then we are doomed to live in the overcautious world of boredom. **Arthur Koestler** once said, "If the creator had a purpose in equipping us with a neck, he surely meant us to stick it out."

T.S. Eliot said, "Only those who risk going too far can possibly find out how far they can go."

Faith is spelt "R-I-S-K". It was who God created us to have nobility and a powerful sense of curiosity. God created us to explore. God created us to handle risk. We were built for challenge. We were built for bravery. We were built for greatness. We were built for weathering great storms coming through and finding victory in seeming defeat.

When we identify this need in the hearts of men, is it any wonder why the Church puts men off Jesus? Guys are looking for adventure, a bit of testosterone, an atmosphere where they can "bloke it out" with other guys.

William Shedd, nineteenth century professor of English literature once said, "A ship is safe in harbour, but that's not what ships are for."

There is an old African proverb too that says: "Smooth seas do not make skilful sailors."

An even older Chinese proverb says: "We cannot discover new oceans until we have the courage to lose sight of the shore."

Man Shall Not Live on Girls Alone
The Starship Enterprise and her crew were never meant for safe harbours, but for the risk involved in carrying out their primary mandate. Similarly, we as human beings are not satisfied unless we

are actively involved in pursuing risk, without it we settle for monotony, we descend into tedium and live life bored to death.

Is it possible God could be speaking through Hollywood? In **Matthew 13**, Jesus explained to the people around Him that He would only speak in parables, that He couldn't communicate deep spiritual truth any other way and this is why He chose stories with spiritual truth.

Could it be possible that God is communicating with our modern world through some of the stories we see on TV and the silver screen? I believe God has not forsaken Hollywood – I believe the signs of His presence are obvious.

Take care you don't allow scepticism to silence His voice. Make sure you take time for a closer look; take care you don't allow cynicism or disillusionment with the traditional Church to make you blind to His activity in the world today. Take care to not let the human condition of pride and arrogance rob you of an experience with God.

Aristotle, an ancient Greek philosopher, once said: "Adventure is worthwhile."

Why do men like these kinds of movies? Why do we watch with a sense of excitement? Have you ever wondered what makes a great guy flick? Think about it. Guys love movies with big guns, fast cars, fights scenes, dumb jokes and huge explosions. Someone must die, even if it is only on the big screen!

British mathematician, **Alfred Whitehead**, once said: "Without adventure, civilization is in full decay." For a mathematician that's an important principle! It's true, "Man shall not live by girls alone" – we need adventure!

To actually qualify as a guy flick or "man movie", the movie should make men want to watch it again and again, learn the lines, and quote them whenever possible. When a guy does blurt one of them out in public, it should make other guys, total strangers even, glance over at him and nod with respect.

I have always been adventurous. I would prefer to throw caution to the wind whenever possible. I'll usually try most things once! I really experience this with food; I have eaten dog, snake, camel, raw fish, whale, puffin, seal, reindeer, venison, frog, snails, alligator and crocodile, kangaroo, witchetty grubs, buffalo, raw octopus, fish head curry, and fish dipped in ground bugs guts mixed with chillies.

John Eldredge says "Adventure is written into the heart of every man and it cries out to be fulfilled." Adventure is important because it has the ability to put men to the test, and though we may fear the test, at the same time we yearn to be tested to discover that we have what it takes!

I have discovered there is something **fierce in the heart of every man**. It is competitive, spirited and ready for action. It wants fun and to pit itself against others whether on the sports field, the court at Wimbledon or while playing on a Wii. Most guys only need a bit of egging on and they will be in to the fray. If there are a bunch of guys together near a swimming pool – someone will be thrown in.

God has placed this adventure into every man's heart. **Psalms 139:13-14** says, "For you created my inmost being; you knit me together in my mother's womb. I praise you because I am fearfully and wonderfully made; your works are wonderful, I know that full well."

- **Fearfully:** created to inspire fear, dangerously made, made to inspire reverence, my creation would cause awe and wonder in the hearts of others.
- **Wonderfully:** distinguished, notably made, famously created, renown, prominent; created to be a hero, well known for the eminence of my creation.

- **Your works are wonderful:** I don't believe God is speaking of a macho man, but a real man, a genuine man, the real article. We were created to be like Christ. Never forget it, our need for adventure is to always be realised with integrity and righteousness.

What happens when this sense of adventure is ignored or repressed? What happens when this yearning for adventure is disregarded or allowed to be restrained? It breaks out in good natured fun and valiant exploit. It is this need for adventure that can produce heroes or villains. The need for adventure can produce people of integrity and character or sometimes it breaks out in infidelity, drunkenness, immorality, seduction and, many times, in violence.

The heart cries out for adventure, for exploits of bravery and courage. The heart cries to **distinguish itself**, it is a deep cry placed there by God. It is a need that if repressed, emasculated or ignored will break out.

Have you ever wondered what God thinks of this need for adventure? If I am correct it was Him who put it there and it will be God who shows us how to express this deep cry of the human heart.

This reminds me of my adventure days in Alice Springs: There was camel racing in forty five degree temperatures, the Henley on Todd Regatta which was the dry river boat race, climbing Ayers Rock, swimming in Mataranka hot springs. For me it was walking in Kakadu National Park and swimming in Katherine Gorge (with crocodiles!); driving for miles on end from Alice to Darwin (1,500 kilometres!). Is it any wonder why the Bible tells and retells stories of adventure, of daring, of brave deeds and heroism?

This is the reason I did TWO "Tough Mudder" events – one in 2013 one in 2014. Tough Mudder is a 12 mile 25 obstacle course. When you complete it you earn a headband! YEAH!! HOORAH!! I competed in Spartan Race late in 2015 and another in 2016!! Adventure is bound up in the heart of men!

We Were Created for Adventure
This is why a lot of men don't like Church. It's just all too safe for them; too feminine. To most men God is either distant or weak; the very thing men report of their own earthly fathers.

One guy said to me the other day in describing Jesus, "He's a nice guy surrounded by kids, sort of a Mother Teresa type person."

John Eldredge says in *Wild at Heart*: "And when Christ returns, He is at the head of a dreadful company, mounted on a white horse, with a double edged sword, his robe dipped in blood. Now that sounds a lot more like William Wallace than it does Mother Teresa."

There is something fierce in the heart of God and His deep cries to our deep. This need in every man's heart is meant to breakout in all manner of excitement and exhilaration. It is our need for adventure, to do exploits in the name of our God, to find and fulfil destiny, to be part of something bigger than ourselves to carry a vision that will take us a life time to achieve, to serve the living God and honour and live for Him.

The deepest cry of the human heart is for connection with God; to boldly go where no man has gone before!

Jewish authors would never have invented either that style or that morality; and the Gospel has marks of truth so great, so striking, so utterly inimitable, that the invention of it would be more astonishing than the hero. **Jean Jacques Rousseau, French sceptic.**

Most people are bothered by those passages of Scripture they do not understand, but the passages that bother me are those I do understand. **Mark Twain.**

The word of God hidden in the heart is a stubborn voice to suppress. **Billy Graham.**

Chapter 14: *The Book of Eli* – Jesus and the End of the World

The story line is simple and not too unbelievable; the scene is set in post-apocalyptic America. An atomic war left the Earth shattered and the environment destroyed. The film centres on one man a guy called Eli played by Denzel Washington. He believes he's heard the voice of God to go west and carry with him the last existing copy of the King James Bible.

He meets a guy called Carnegie played by Gary Oldman in a town with no name; this guy is sort of like a warlord over the city and is in desperate search of a Bible. He says this book has the power to restore order and it has power and will give him authority. To cut a long story short, Oldman has a fight with Denzel and takes the Bible from him.

At the end of the movie, Carnegie is with his copy of the scriptures trying to open it and Eli finally makes it west to San Francisco (or what's left of it) and is severely wounded. Now I'm gonna ruin a great flick... I'm so sorry for those of you who have seen this movie. Carnegie finally opens the Bible and finds it is in written in braille!

Eli is on Alcatraz Island; we then discover he is blind! (I watched the movie a few times and it's consistent throughout the movie – Denzel really does act like a blind guy!) But here's the real power of the movie; he tells the guy on Alcatraz to get some paper, a lot of paper and he starts to quote back to him the entire Bible starting in Genesis 1! The end of the movie is seen with Denzel laying back now nice and clean and **he has, from memory, quoted the whole Bible!**

I find this amazing that Hollywood would make a movie that places the word of God is such a powerful light! To me, this movie screams that God has not forsaken this world, that God has not left the world to its own devices! To me it shouts out that God is speaking to the world and He has used Hollywood to make His voice heard! (I'm so sorry for all the exclamation marks but this movie really is one out of the bag!)

The power of this movie is not that Eli was blind, not that the world had destroyed itself, not even the resilience of man to rebuild. But the main point is the power of the Word of God; and that a man could memorise the entire Bible.

I know it's Hollywood but hey, that's why its location is America and there is so much fighting and ridiculous one liners. But whoa... what a thought - memorising the entire Bible, that's amazing!

In my early Christian walk (I'd only been a believer for maybe a few months), we began to seriously memorise the key verses in the Bible. In my early days I had a Thompson Chain Reference Bible made from thick leather. It was a very serious and formidable Bible for such a young convert. My friends and I were so passionate; we had found The Lord! Hallelujah! We were "Jesus Freaks". We were radicals. We listened to Christian rock 'n' roll. We were fanatics about Jesus and shared His message with whoever would listen and we were always quoting the Bible; I mean *always* quoting the Bible.

We were passionate about our first love; Jesus, and realised we needed to feed on His word daily. And we did just that! Even though my brain had been scrambled by drugs and I could barely tell you my

Plain View

address, I could quote large portions of scripture! It is amazing the power of the word of God.

What are your feelings about the Bible? It's too hard to understand, it's boring. There's too much history, it's too big a book. I don't know where to start; why are there so many translations? But the Bible is the source book that explains to us who Jesus Christ is and how we can know God. It is not only an important historical book but it is God's word to the world.

"Your word is a lamp to my feet and a light for my path." **Psalms 119:105**

God's word is like a lamp and it is a light that shines to show the way. All you need in life for guidance, direction, health, peace, understanding and illumination is found in God's word. God's word illuminates our world. It is spiritual food that not only sustains us but prospers us in every way.

One of my favourite parts of the movie *Eli* is when Denzel and the girl ((Mila Kunis) are walking out in the desert and she asks this question:

Solara: You know, you say you've been walking for thirty years, right?
Eli: Right.
Solara: Have you ever thought that maybe you were lost?
Eli: Nope.
Solara: Well, how do you know that you're walking in the right direction?
Eli: I walk by faith, not by sight.
Solara: [*sighs*] What does that mean?
Eli: It means that you know something even if you don't know something.
Solara: That doesn't make any sense.
Eli: It doesn't have to make sense. It's faith, it's faith. It's the flower of light in the field of darkness that's giving me the strength to carry on. You understand?

Solara: Is that from your book?
Eli: No, it's, uh, Johnny Cash, Live at Folsom Prison.

He is quoting from **2 Corinthians 5:7** as well as Johnny Cash![129]

There is no book like The Bible in all of history. It stands unique in all of the world. It is the most shop lifted item on the planet! Fifty copies of it are published every minute, making it the most popular book in the entire history of publishing. The Bible has the distinction of being the first book to ever be published!

The Bible is Inspired by God
"Above all, you must understand that no prophecy of Scripture came about by the prophet's own interpretation. For prophecy never had its origin in the will of man, but men spoke from God as they were carried along by the Holy Spirit." **2 Peter 1:20-21**

"All Scripture is God-breathed and is useful for teaching, rebuking, correcting and training in righteousness, so that the man of God may be thoroughly equipped for every good work."
2 Timothy 3:16-17

On the website for my church we record our statement of faith, it says this: "We believe the Bible is God's Word. It is inspired, infallible, accurate, authoritative and applicable to our everyday lives."

Infallible: Perfect - Reliable - Dependable - Flawless; without fault and accurate. It is authoritative like nothing else. No other written or spoken word comes anywhere near the power of the word of God. It may have been written 3,500 years ago but it more relevant today than the breaking news on BBC.

"Your word, O LORD, is eternal; it stands firm in the heavens." **Psalms 119:89**

---

[129] Greystone Chapel by Glen Sherley, performed by Johnny Cash at Folsom Prison

Plain View

Jesus said in **Matthew 4:4**: ""It is written: 'Man does not live on bread alone, but on every word that comes from the mouth of God.'""

The word of God is more vital to us than physical food. If you want to understand how to hear the voice of God; then read the Bible and you'll hear His voice. I'm tired of super-spiritual flaky rubbish; if you want to hear God's voice, then read His word. Too often we're waiting for a "word from God" when we already have a word from God; the Bible.

"For the word of God is living and active. Sharper than any double-edged sword, it penetrates even to dividing soul and spirit, joints and marrow; it judges the thoughts and attitudes of the heart." **Hebrews 4:12**

Read it, live according to it, memorise it, mediate on it daily, hide it in your heart, write it out, break it down to understand it, get some Bible tools like a concordance, lexicons, commentaries and Greek and Hebrew explanations.

Imagine a Church solid, Bible based and touching the community. We say all the time "it's the word of God that has the power to change your life." Then read it, memorise it, learn it and live by it. God's word will change our city as we live it out right in front of them. People will say, "What is it about you?" We become letters seen and read of all men (**2 Corinthians 3:2**).

The Bible is the book that reveals who Jesus is. It doesn't matter how contemporary you are, how modern your Church is or how up to date you try to make your church services; without the word of God being proclaimed and explained you are just having a concert.

The Bible is the revelation of Jesus Christ and takes over where common grace leaves off. Jesus is described as "the Word of God." The only way we can connect people with Jesus is by the preaching, teaching and communicating of the word of God. There is no other way. I don't care what the movie is or the song lyric says, if it doesn't introduce the word of God all you've become is a movie reviewer and not a proclaimer of God's eternal truth.

If you've had the courage to read this far, know this; I believe in the word of God. I also believe we must find practical and contemporary ways to tell people what it says. The word of God is the lamp that reveals Jesus and brings Him out from the shadow of ignorance. The word of God is a light to showcase the beauty and power of Jesus, without the word of God being proclaimed and creatively communicated, this world is lost in ignorance.

Winston Churchill once said, "The truth is incontrovertible, malice may attack it, ignorance may deride it, but in the end; there it is."

Evil is a point of view. We are immortal. And what we have before us are the rich feasts that conscience cannot appreciate and mortal men cannot know without regret. God kills, and so shall we; indiscriminately He takes the richest and the poorest, and so shall we; for no creatures under God are as we are, none so like Him as ourselves, dark angels not confined to the limits of Hell but wandering His Earth and all its kingdoms. **Vampire Lestat from *Interview with a Vampire* by Anne Rice.**

I decided as long as I was going to Hell, I might as well do it thoroughly. **Edward Cullen from *Twilight* by Stephenie Meyer.**

There are few nudities so objectionable as the naked truth. **Agnes Repplier (1855 –1950).**

Truth is beautiful, without doubt; but so are lies. **Ralph Waldo Emerson.**

Chapter 15: The *Twilight* Phenomena... what the heck is going on?

One of my dear friends encouraged me to NOT include this chapter. He says, "Tom, there is a line and you don't need to cross over it!" He encouraged me to "... leave out the vampire stuff." I thought it through but felt it was an important thing happening in pop culture and it begged to be addressed; so here it is!

I am simply amazed by the number of vampire, werewolf, witch and occult movies there are today: *Vampire Diaries, The Originals, True Blood, Penny Dreadful,* and the countless remakes of *Dracula*; not to mention the band called *Vampire Weekend* and the list goes on!

You have *Teen Wolf,* a teenage TV series about a high school teenager becoming a werewolf. There's *The Secret Circle* where a group of teenagers explore their witchcraft powers. There is the TV series that has literally taken the world by storm - *The Walking Dead*, a TV series about zombies!

Media is being inundated with TV series about supernatural beings (who all look like us and go to high school). Critically acclaimed new TV series, *An American Horror Story* staring Lady Gaga has every one getting excited as a haunted house does its thing! There's the series *Grimm*, a new take on Grimm's Fairy tales where they're not stories but warnings!

There are even some big screen offerings over the last decade like the *Twilight Saga* about werewolves and vampires. Brad Pitt's company even bought the movie rights to a 2006 book called *WW Z: an oral history of the Zombie Wars*, he used Glasgow as one of the locations.

I think something's going on and the Church needs to sit up and really listen. Something big, brash and shockingly spiritual is happening in the world around us and we need to stop and take a closer look. I believe this is **the most *profound, provocative, and exciting expressions of legitimate spiritual yearning in at least 100 years.***

And it is!
Not everyone enjoys this kind of TV; my friend Jon Cook said, "*Twilight* is like *Dawson's Creek* meets *Dracula*; a complete waste of time." In the immortal word of Robert Redford, "*Twilight* is for wimps; vampires and pretty boys!" When asked if he wanted to see the latest *Twilight* movie, Jon Cook said he would prefer to put his iPad into a meat grinder; I personally thought that was a bit excessive.

Now don't get me wrong, I do not endorse the morality or the spirituality of every movie or book I read. Nor would I endorse the violence and senseless killings; but I am mature enough to differentiate between fact and fiction, Hollywood and real life, myths and legends as opposed to the reality of everyday life. To be a modern day commentator of pop culture you need to be mature and discerning as well. But in your attempts to be discerning don't throw out the "baby with the bath water".

What gets me about the *Twilight* movies; it's is not the love between two people, err.... or was that three people? It's not the struggles between good and evil; not the morality and "wholesomeness" of some of the characters. What gets me about these movies is that the foundation, the very basis for them is a total fabrication; it's a lie. These creatures don't exist! It's a lie. Whoa... hang on I know this is a novel idea for some but it's true – vampires do not exist, there are no werewolves and zombies are not real! There I said it!

Sorry, there is no such thing as bloodsucking skin walkers. There are no "walkers" or living dead amongst us, there is no such thing as vampires; they are mythological creatures, they are folklore; a result of man's dark and fearful imagination, werewolves too... they only exist in the imagination of others. Not real!

Yet the idea of vampires has captured the imagination of thousands, I suppose it springs from the desire to live forever. Even that is a lie. People don't live forever surviving on the blood of other humans. Now I know that most of you believe this. You're not fooled by this – hey? (Just checking!) You can separate fantasy and facts; can't you? You know, just like my Daddy said, "Boy, that's just Hollywood!" [130]

I like the part in the movie *Twilight* where Bella and Edward are talking about him being a Vampire; Bella gets a look at Edward's skin in the sun. (And I thought vampires couldn't stand the sun! Thanks Stephenie.)

Bella: It's like diamonds... you're beautiful.
Edward: Beautiful? This is the skin of a killer, Bella... I'm a killer!

---

[130] Bobby Rawls – 1928 – 2008; thought you should know since I told you my mother's name.

Bella: I don't believe that.

Edward: That's because *you believe only the lies*... the camouflage. I'm the world's most dangerous predator, Bella. Everything about me invites you in; my voice, my face, even my smell. As if I would need any of that... as if you could out run me... as if you could fight me off. I'm designed to kill.

Bella: I don't care.

Edward: I've killed people before.

Bella: It doesn't matter.

Edward: I wanted to kill you at first. I've never wanted a human's blood so much, before.

Bella: I trust you.

Edward: Don't.

"You believe only the lie... the camouflage." Not everyone can differentiate between truth and lies. Has anyone seen the TV series, *Lie to me?*[131] Brilliant stuff and the science behind it is true. But what happens when we tell lies to ourselves?

Did you know there are people even today who actually believe in vampires? There are people who so want to become a vampire that they file their teeth to sharp points and even drink blood. I've heard there is a local pub where you can purchase blood. This is a powerful lie to believe.

The Bible has something to say about lies and believing lies; in **2 Thessalonians 2:10-11** there is, embedded in this passage, a powerful concept. Listen to this; "[People] perish because they refused to love the truth and so be saved. For this reason God sends them a powerful delusion so that they will believe the lie ..."

---

[131] Tim Roth who plays the character of Dr Cal Lightman who interprets micro-expressions, through the Facial Action Coding System, and body language. The science is real, the story lines fabricated.

Plain View

Listen to this passage, "People perish because they refuse to love the truth." This is a shock to all those Universalists out there who somehow believe that love wins and everybody gets to go to Heaven. Not true.

What is a lie? *Dictionary.com* says a lie is a "false statement made with deliberate intent to deceive; an intentional untruth." A lie is something intended to convey a false impression. A lie is an inaccurate or false statement.

When faced with truth, people will at times refuse to recognise, accept or acknowledge it, preferring the route of least resistance. The consequence is that they "perish" or don't succeed because they believed a lie. The ultimate end for those who believe the lie is an eternity without Christ, in a place the Bible calls Hell. It is the awful end for those who reject Jesus Christ, the Truth.

Because people refuse the truth, God gives them up to their system of error. If a man strongly prefers error to truth then it's not wrong, from anyone's point of view, to allow him to freely demonstrate his own preference for the lie.

"They exchanged the truth of God for a lie, and worshipped and served created things rather than the Creator." **Romans 1:25**

Here is the crux; when you believe a lie, you allow a lie to be regarded as truth. To you, the lie is true. Like I said; I know a lot of people who believe in vampires but believing a lie doesn't make it true. It doesn't matter how sincerely you believe a lie, it is still a lie, it doesn't matter how many people believe the lie - it doesn't make it true.

At one time, a lot of people believed the world was flat. That didn't make it right; even though at one time the Church steadfastly believed the world was flat. That still didn't make the lie a truth.

Believing the Lie...

I know of a lot of people who believe lies; lies about themselves, lies about other people, lies about what the Bible says and lies about God. Just because you believe a lie to be true doesn't make it true. This point is very powerful, listen; you can believe a lie and it becomes truth to you. You act on it; you trust it and the lie influences and impacts your life. You interact with the lies but that still doesn't mean it is a truth. If you act on information that is not true but you *believe* to be true, it does impact you - but not like the way truth will impact you.

A lie holds you captive; a lie imprisons you with its falsehood. A lie confines you and restricts your ability to respond. A lie keeps you in the dark, keeps you restrained and keeps you limited and cramped! A lie is no foundation to build on. A lie is a false piece of information that, if received, can destroy you.

"Then you will know the truth, and the truth will set you free." **John 8:32**

People lie to themselves all the time:
- "Outside circumstances determine my life and future." Not true, it's the way I respond to the world around me that determines my future; my destiny is not what happens to me but is determined by how I respond to what happens to me.
- "I need to be beautiful, thin and dress well for people to like me." Not true, what I look like doesn't attract people to me, it's who I am that people find attractive.
- When men get together, how do they define themselves? The answer is "by what we do" – but this is not true. We are not defined by what we do, but by who we are!

Our feelings lie to us all the time:
- "If I feel something then it must be true." Not true, your feelings will lie to you and we need to be able to differentiate between what our feelings say and what is truth.
- "If I feel unloved, then I must be."

Plain View

- "If I'm feeling worthless, then I must be."
- "If I feel God has deserted me, then what's the use of praying?"
- "If I feel like life is hopeless, then it must be."
- "I feel down and a million miles away from God, He must have abandoned me."
- "I feel insecure, so I won't try, I won't have a go – what's the use, I'll only fail again."
- "I feel ugly, I feel depressed, I feel stupid, I feel defeated and I feel ready to give up."

There are some people who tell lies about us:
- People make up stuff about you.
- People start false stories or rumours about you that put you in a bad light.
- People say evil things about you that are not true and their words hurt.
- People make up things about you that are not true, some of that stuff finds its way into the media and on the Internet – people tells lies about you that others BELIEVE!

"Reckless words pierce like a sword." **Proverbs 12:18**

"I am in the midst of lions; I lie among ravenous beasts, men whose teeth are spears and arrows, whose tongues are sharp swords." **Psalms 57:4**

Sometimes we believe lies about God!
- "When I become a Christian nothing bad will ever happen to me."
- "When I am one of God's children, everything I ask for in prayer will be given to me."
- "Now I am a Christian, I will live in harmony with all of God's other children!"
- "Now God lives in me I will not ever go through another trial or tough situation."

The consequence of believing lies is too great! Lies impact us in negative ways

Have you believed a lie about God?
- "God couldn't love me."
- "God couldn't forgive all my sins – I'm too bad."
- "God won't want anything to do with me until I can clean myself up a bit – you know get my act together first."
- "God's not real; God's not interested in the world."
- "God hates me, God is punishing me, God is angry at me."
- "I'm so sinful, God couldn't come anywhere near me; I am so unworthy of God's love!"

Here is the truth; **John 3:15-17**, "For God loved the world so much that he gave his only Son so that anyone who believes in him shall not perish but have eternal life. God did not send his Son into the world to condemn it, but to save it."

Here is the truth; in **John 17:17**, Jesus says, "Your word is truth", speaking of the Bible.

To fight is a radical instinct; if men have nothing else to fight over they will fight over words, fancies, or women; or they will fight because they dislike each other's looks, or because they have met walking in opposite directions. **George Santayana (1863-1952), Spanish born American Philosopher, Poet and Humanist.**

Let us therefore brace ourselves to our duty, and so bear ourselves that if the British Empire and its Commonwealth last for a thousand years, men will still say, "This was their finest hour." **Winston Churchill (1874-1965).**

While women weep, as they do now, I'll fight; while children go hungry, as they do now I'll fight; while men go to prison, in and out, in and out, as they do now, I'll fight; while there is a drunkard left, while there is a poor lost girl upon the streets, while there remains one dark soul without the light of God, I'll fight, I'll fight to the very end! **William Booth, founder of the Salvation Army.**

Chapter 16: *Gladiator* - The Cry of the Human Heart to Fight

"What we do in life echoes in eternity!" - Maximus, *Gladiator.*

2 Timothy 4:7 says "I have fought the good fight, I have finished the race, I have kept the faith."

Knitted, interwoven and bound into the fabric of every human heart is a cry to fight! The cry to fight is in our nature, it is intrinsic to the makeup of humanity. Connected with this call to fight there is courage, bravery and heroism. There is also pettiness, meanness and low down nastiness. We choose what we will fight for, but believe me; we were created to fight!

Exodus 15:3 says "The LORD is a warrior; the LORD is his name."

In the film *Gladiator*, Australian, Russell Crowe plays the lead role of General **Maximus Decimus Meridius** who serves Emperor **Marcus**

Aurelius as Rome's greatest general. The Emperor is old and wants Maximus to succeed him as Emperor but Marcus Aurelius' son **Commodus** finds out and murders his father and takes the throne of Rome! Maximus finds out and refuses to serve the new Emperor.

Commodus is a weak willed and unprincipled man who fights dirty. He is seditious, he is a murderer and he is corrupt and devious. He decides to eliminate Maximus but, through a series of events, Maximus escapes his death sentence and makes his way back to his home only to find that Commodus has murdered his family and burned his home and fields. Now, nearly dead from a wound sustained in his escape, a band of slave traders find him and take him into captivity.

Maximus goes on to become a first century celebrity as the slave/gladiator who thrills Rome and then later faces Commodus and defies an empire! The movie vividly contrasts Maximus and Commodus; in their character and how they fight.

It is a historical story and a fascinating movie, full of action. Once again it's a real man movie with many great and gory fight scenes. There are no car chases though, no shoot outs ... but there are horses, man's best friend after dog, and did I mention loads of fighting?! The name *Gladiator* makes it clear there is a lot of fighting and ... many people die; but hey, it's a guy flick and it's Hollywood!

I've always been more of a lover than a fighter. But I do remember a fight I had in high school. It was me and my best friend Darryl. For whatever reason, we started to annoy each other and before long it turned into pushing and shoving. He threw a punch and I returned fire. Before we knew it, we were wrestling each other on the ground and a crowd had gathered. The bell rang for the end of lunch and we decided it was over; we were still best friends.

I remember another quite interesting time. I was living in Melbourne, Australia and was attending a pastor's day at a local church. I was still trying out a few looks as I was pastoring an interesting church in Melbourne. We had punks, goths and heavy metal aficionados so I was experimenting with hair dye! I had dyed my hair a combination of red and black and it included my beard!

One pastor, who I didn't like very much because of his constant sarcasm, came up to me and started to make fun of me. What should I do? I had coloured my hair and beard so I'd better "take it like a man." That is until he decided to pull my beard while saying, "Oh, so you've dyed your beard too?"

I don't know what took over me but I immediately reached my right hand up and grabbed his arm which was attached to his hand still pulling on my beard and said, "Touch me like that one more time and I'll smack the crap out of you. Now let go of my beard, punk!" (Shades of Clint Eastwood!) He paled. He let go and he never bothered me again! I felt good. (I'm not even going to try and justify myself here, it happened as I said it did, get over it.)

You know what it means as well; won't you fight for something important?

We Will All Be Stirred By a Noble Cause
There's the speech made by Churchill, "We will fight them on the beaches..."

There's the speech by William Wallace before the battle of Stirling, "Sons of Scotland..."

There's the Martin Luther King speech, "I have a dream ..."

Every one of us can be stirred by a noble cause! And we will fight!

We fight for our children if there is injustice, especially where there is bullying or where there are teachers lacking in integrity. We fight where ever we sense injustice, unfairness or inequality.

We'll fight for our nation during a time of war. We'll fight for those in need and those who are less fortunate. We'll fight to help those unable to fight. We'll fight for good and noble causes; maybe even our hair colour!

But our greatest fights are on the inside of us!

David McKay, author and religious leader, once said: "The most important of life's battles is the one we fight daily in the silent chambers of the soul."

There are times we will need to fight through our own personal battles. In the silent chambers of our soul there will be the battle over destructive thoughts; there are ideas we cherish about ourselves that seek to debilitate us...

Sally Kempton, author once said; "It's hard to fight an enemy who has outposts in your head."

The cry of the human heart is to fight; not give up! None of us have been called to give up; we were not created for defeat.

A young man by the name of Jonah Mowry[132] posted a video in late 2011 that went viral; in the video he said he would not consider suicide as an answer to his difficulties. He wrote, "I have a million reasons to live; I AM STRONGER THAN THIS!" This boy is fighting... fighting for his own life!

This internal desire to fight may have been dampened by political correctness and we sometimes simmer on the inside because we think it's not appropriate to be seen as aggressively going after what we want. So we just lie down and die; we give up, we surrender to an unjust force, it irks us on the inside, we get irritated and soon we

---

[132] You Tube video by Jonah Mowry "What's going on?" - well worth a watch. At the time of publishing his video had recorded over 8 million hits!

just become compliant and keep quiet. This is not what God has created us for – we were created for victory; we were created to fight and win!

Tacitus, a Roman senator once said, "A desire to resist oppression is implanted in the nature of man." He spoke truth. I'm glad Jonah listened too, the world is a richer place because of this young man!

Our fighting, though, should never come down to the level of a street fight; we are created not to squabble or quarrel, not to bicker and fall out with each other, not to waste our time in meaningless arguing and not to just fight for the sake of fighting. It is not noble to fight according to our own selfish, self-serving agendas; no, we fight on a much grander scale.

Some of us think we wouldn't fight at all, but put a child in danger, and we will fight. Not only will our heart lead us into the battle but we will distinguish ourselves as heroes.

Aristotle once said, "We become brave by doing brave acts."
I believe that common mortal men shed their disguise and become heroes when they fight for what is noble, for what is right and for what is just and good.

What *Gladiator* reveals and exposes is a deep and primal cry of the human heart to fight! We will fight for revenge or we'll fight for justice; we will fight for vanity or we will fight for what is right; but we will fight.

But what does God have to say about the primal human cry in our hearts to fight?

It is no secret; the cry of the human heart is to fight. It's a primal, primitive and ancient principle laid there by God for our protection. **Ephesians 6:10-12** says "Finally, be strong in the Lord and in his mighty power. Put on the full armour of God so that you can take your stand against the devil's schemes. For our struggle is not against flesh and blood, but against the rulers, against the authorities, against the powers of this dark world and against the spiritual forces of evil in the heavenly realms."

Sometimes our walk with God feels like a fight; and it is. In this scripture God is telling us to be strong in Him and His power; to literally become the Devil's worst nightmare! To put on the full armour of God; take your stand against all the Devil's schemes, plans, plots and conspiracies.

Paul goes on to say our struggle is not against "flesh and blood." This always comes like a surprise to us because the battle really looks like flesh and blood; it looks like my mother in law, my son or daughter. It looks like the boss at work, sometimes it looks just like my professor at school. So often the fight just looks so much like "flesh and blood!" But Paul says it's not! Our struggle, our fight is against the powers of this dark world and against spiritual forces of evil in the heavenly places. We are involved in a spiritual war, it is a spiritual battle.

It's the battle to renew our minds, to change the way we think about ourselves because the Devil wants us to think we are crap, the Devil wants us to think we are fat, stupid and ugly.

The Devil's natural enemy is not God; no fight there. The Devil was defeated and thrown from Heaven eons ago; there is no dark force to counter God's light force! The Devil's natural enemy is US! He hates us and is jealous of us, he seeks to destroy the very image of God within us! He loathes you and me; we are the object of his greatest hatred, and he detests us, can't stand us, despises us and abhors us. But hey, that's okay – I'm not too fond of him either! **It is for this reason we are called upon by God to "take our stand against him!"**[133]

---

[133] Ephesians 6:11

Plain View

We are not left weak and vulnerable either; according to **2 Corinthians 10:4**, "The weapons we fight with are not the weapons of the world. On the contrary, they have divine power to demolish strongholds." We have access to weaponry more powerful than anything this world has seen – we have weapons that are divinely empowered to demolish strong holds!

- Divinely – God has made them available to us.
- Empowered – they have real power.
- Demolish – not just make a mark, not just scratch the enemy or just to draw blood but to completely destroy whatever it is he has build against us.

Sometimes we find ourselves in an unwinnable fight. No matter how we look at it, the enemy is too big, too well resourced and too strong for us. At times we think, "I'll fight any way, even if I'm destined to lose." But there is another way of looking at this spirit to fight.

God says that there will be times when He will fight with us and even fight for us! The scripture says in **Exodus 15:3**: "The LORD is a warrior; the LORD is his name." **Deuteronomy 3:22** continues "Do not be afraid of them; the LORD your God himself will fight for you."

One of the greatest stories ever told in the Bible is the one about David and the giant called Goliath. Just before David goes into battle he says, in **1 Samuel 17:47**, "All those gathered here will know that it is not by sword or spear that the LORD saves; for the battle is the LORD's, and he will give all of you into our hands."

There is one who has also gone on to fight for our salvation, His name is Jesus. In this circumstance you don't need to fight you only need to surrender to God and just be still and receive this great salvation on offer from God. You can trust the One who said, in **Hebrews 13:5-6**, ""Never will I leave you; never will I forsake you.""

Jesus fought an incredible battle to win us over to Him and His love. He fought to win men's hearts and He fought so we could experience His salvation. Through Jesus' fight we have become "more than conquerors through Him who loved us!"[134]

---

[134] Romans 8:37

The purpose of human life is to serve, and to show compassion and the will to help others.
Albert Schweitzer

I work really hard at trying to see the big picture and not getting stuck in ego. I believe we're all put on this planet for a purpose, and we all have a different purpose... When you connect with that love and that compassion, that's when everything unfolds.
Ellen DeGeneres

Galatians 5:15 *New Living Translation, "But if you are always biting and devouring one another, watch out! Beware of destroying one another."*

Chapter 17: *The Walking Dead* – a search for purpose and meaning

One of the most popular TV shows for the last 6 seasons has been **The Walking Dead.** It's a TV show about the end of the world and a survivor's guide to fighting zombies. This TV show is not for the faint of heart! The series has won many awards and its popularity has fascinated me. The TV series had ***12.4 million viewers*** for its season 3 finale, **17.3 million** for season 5 and **14.6 million** to season 6! It was the most-watched drama series telecast in cable history.

I want to make it clear here, "I hate Zombies!"

Maybe we should take a long and thoughtful look at this TV show - is the Holy Spirit stirring something in people's heart? Why are people watching this show? What is it about this show that has people addicted? What tensions are being created in the hearts of people that only Jesus can answer and satisfy?

I have a list of answers:
1.   People love being scared to death – it tells them they are alive!

2. People are fascinated by apocalyptic accounts about the end of the world.
3. People love a good story! We like to identify with various characters.
4. The characters in this TV show are fighting an enemy which they cannot really stop - there's too many of them!!
5. People relate to the hopelessness of their plight!
6. People are cheering on the survivors hoping they make it - we love an underdog and hate it when one of our favourite characters is bitten by a zombie!
7. People see the horror of these zombies and we will do anything to not let it happen to us!

Zombies are technically reanimated corpses - but they are bereft of consciousness and self-awareness. They are the walking dead, biters, or walkers. They act according to a thoughtless instinct to kill and destroy those who are alive. They exist to eat the flesh of the living and in turn their victims become like them - one bite and BOOM you become a zombie. Frightening stuff.

There is a fascination with zombies as anti-heroes. We hate them, yet we are fascinated by them. From an entertainment point of view we love the darkness and the horror of these pesky creatures but we never want to be like them. We don't want to become a zombie!! We hate what they represent but secretly fear we might become like them!! This scares us to death.

This TV show plays on one of our greatest human fears; that we might live wasted lives, aimlessly wandering with no direction, trivializing ourselves into silliness and confusion. One of our deep fears is that we become thoughtless or enter into a mindless existence with no sense of destiny. We fear the revelation that we have no sense of direction left in our lives.

We fear we might miss our destiny, our sense of purpose and our glorious sense of potential to achieve great things in this world. We fear we may never see our dreams fulfilled and that we will never make our mark on history.

The older we become the more pronounced this feeling becomes. This feeling takes a hold of us. We suffer from midlife crises, birthday blues or slight depression as we age; wondering with a sense of anxiety if we'll ever achieved anything worthy of note.

We never want to become a zombie; a thoughtless, mindless, passionless animated corpse. We don't ever want to become simply a walker who shuffles through life with no feeling - no thoughts, no self-awareness, no conscious thoughts and no actual goals - aimlessly wandering unable to live and unable to die.

We fear our natural laziness and our innate lack of enthusiasm will leave us with no drive, no ambition, no motivation and no energy to live this life. We fear we will miss out on God's plan for our lives shambling through life because of our apathy and lethargy. Some people have simply given up - this is status quo for them – this has become the horrifying reality for some!

Many fear they will be entombed in this animated corpse with no drive. Instead of achievement, instead of fulfilling dreams and destiny, we, out of our insecurity, find ourselves criticising anyone else who seems to be different and actually achieving something in their life. The horror of this is that some have simply settled for a life just as I have described.

As **Galatians 5:15** says in the New Living Translation, "But if you are always biting and devouring one another, watch out! Beware of destroying one another."

We loathe these zombies and don't want to become like them but ironically we find ourselves giving in to criticism and negativity; biting and devouring one another. We find ourselves entombed in a life with no drive, no ambition and shuffle with an aimlessness similar to these zombies. The best we feel we can do is criticise and trivialise the lives of those who are around us who are trying to achieve something. We bite and devour others instead of seeking to create an alternative.

I haven't found what I'm looking for so you can't either. I haven't achieved my dreams - I feel empty - I feel unfulfilled - my life looks a little meaningless and trivial - so I won't let you feel good about your life!

Because of our own lack of achievement we seek to tear the flesh off others and do it for sport. We bite and devour people. We pull others down and destroy their reputations. We want to have them in our group so we can shuffle together; criticising and trivialising. With neither sense nor direction left in their lives they eat others; some have called it the tall poppy syndrome.

What we don't realise is that what we sow we reap. When we bite and devour others with our mindless criticism, thoughtless censure and aimless denigration of those we don't get or understand we are actually becoming like those zombies who do the same. We are destroying ourselves. Criticism is in fact a self-destructive action.

To make ourselves feel better we feel the need to chase celebrity. We seek for prominence. We hunger for fame. We want to be taken seriously in life but find ourselves willing to short circuit character development and fall for simple self-promotion instead.

Listen to the X Factor contestants - "If I can win this it will change my life forever!" "This is my dream!" Before we condemn these people we need to recognise that within each and every one of us is the desire to achieve something great! Remember God has a destiny and purpose for us to fulfil. God has a plan for our lives. All these X Factor people are articulating is a God given desire to mean something – to have purpose in life.

Plain View

We want to achieve something great in our lives; this desire has been placed there by God. In fact this is what He means when He says He has created *eternity on our hearts* - **Ecclesiastes 3:11** in the Amplified Bible translates it as *[a divinely implanted sense of a purpose working through the ages which nothing under the sun but God alone can satisfy]* It's a hole in our lives that God created and only God can fill. This is a function of our spirit as we were created in the image of God. We were created with purpose by God – in His economy our lives were supposed to count for something.

Yet many live with the fear of a life of anonymity, a life of obscurity - living with a vague sense of "there has to be more than this!" Let's face it, the zombies in this TV show don't talk, they don't carry conversations - there's no specific zombie that has caught our attention - there's no celebrity zombies in *The Walking Dead*! Zombies aren't famous, they will never achieve greatness, they have no dreams and will never make on the cover of *Rolling Stones* magazine!

Our greatest fear is that we, like these anti-celebrity zombies, might be guilty of living a trivial life with no meaning aimlessly shuffling through life hurting people, feeding off people, tearing at their flesh and using people for our own pleasures or for our own gain.

Our greatest fears are that we will be swallowed by our insecurities, drowned by our poor self-image and strangled by our sense of low self-worth. We fear we will be nameless, forgotten, unknown; living lives that are ordinary, mundane and tedious.

When we actually pause and take a long, thoughtful look at this popular TV show we discover that inadvertently people are identifying with this show. On an unconscious and deeper level people are connecting. We hate these loathsome zombies but we hate them because we don't want to become like them.

I've met these people. They are people who may even believe in Jesus but have no passion in their lives. I've met these people. They are aimless, meandering through life. They shuffle through life wandering with no clear direction. They become negative and critical. They end up blaming others for their lack of insight, their lack of maturity and sheer bad luck.

Yes even people who identify with Jesus have fallen for the zombie lifestyle - they are passionless, without a sense of purpose, living without dreams or direction - they have a lifestyle to maintain but lack that sense of destiny! They trivialise themselves into confusion with no sense of direction.

Jesus may even be a part of their life but He's not their everything. They may have a relationship with Jesus but have never discovered His Lordship. They may have been going to church for years but lack the insights of living a life centred on Jesus and His mission in the world.

The answer is Jesus Christ - He is standing in plain view - but many fail to actually follow Him, surrender to Him and sincerely seek to serve Him. They have become strangers to extravagant worship. They are unfamiliar with the sound of His voice mistaking the lure of this world for true riches. They have become foreigners to His word and merely visitors to the weekly gatherings.

The resolution to a zombie lifestyle is to discover Jesus Christ and to love Him and serve Him – *passionately!!* The answer to a zombie attitude towards life is a radical abandonment to the Lordship of Jesus Christ. The final solution to avoiding a zombie way of life is to be passionately connected with Jesus Christ acknowledging Him as King of Kings and Lord of Lords of your life.

The key to living with passion, purpose and direction is to identify strongly with Jesus in His death and to realise that the same spirit who raised Him to life again lives within you!! The solution to

Plain View

trivialising ourselves into silliness and confusion is to acknowledge Jesus Christ as Saviour.

James 4: 7 - 8 says it so clearly, "Submit yourselves, then, to God. Resist the devil, and he will flee from you. Come near to God and He will come near to you. Wash your hands, you sinners, and purify your hearts, you double-minded."

Colossians 1: 10 - 11 "... so that you may live a life worthy of the Lord and please him in every way: bearing fruit in every good work, growing in the knowledge of God, being strengthened with all power according to his glorious might so that you may have great endurance and patience."

The answer to a zombie lifestyle is to be passionately connected to the Risen Lord Jesus Christ. Surrender to His love, give in to His will, yield to His grace and respond to His life in you. Far from being a zombie, God's desire for us is that we become His people - alive, active and full of faith!

The message of the Church today is not about the walking dead but about those who dream with eyes wide open. Today's message is not about the walking dead but about those who are alive. The message of the Church is not about zombies but about living the dream, fulfilling our purpose - discovering our destiny! The message of the Church is not about the end of the world but about becoming the change in the world.

The message of the Church is not about a killer virus that will wipe out the world's population leaving us mindless shuffling corpses; the message today is about connecting with Jesus Christ and His Lordship - surrendering your life to Him and living with passion, enthusiasm and energy.

This is not the end - this is the beginning! The beginning of a new life, a new passion and a new dream!! Live it with Jesus Christ.

Plain View

"If I find in myself desires which nothing in this world can satisfy, the only logical explanation is that I was made for another world." C.S. Lewis, Mere Christianity.

Chapter 18: *Downton Abbey* – A Desire for a Better Life

I want to talk about a TV show that has stirred the desires of a generation. This TV show has fascinated and entertained audiences on both sides of the Atlantic. This TV show has stirred the eternity in the heart of many!

Downton Abbey is a British period drama television series created by Julian Fellowes. It first aired on ITV in the UK on 26 September 2010 and on PBS in the US on 9 January 2011. Its final episode aired the 25th December 2015.

The series, set in the Yorkshire country estate of Downton Abbey, depicts the lives of the aristocratic Crawley family and their servants in post-Edwardian England.

Downton Abbey has received serious acclaim from television critics and won numerous accolades, including a Golden Globe Award for Best Miniseries or Television Film and a Primetime Emmy Award for Outstanding Miniseries or Movie. Many Hollywood stars are asking just how they get a Downtown Abby cameo gig after Shirley MacLaine starred on this popular TV drama.

Downton Abbey was recognised by Guinness World Records as **the most critically acclaimed English-language television series of 2011.** It earned the most nominations of any international television series in the history of the Primetime Emmy Awards. It was the most watched television series on both ITV and PBS, and subsequently became the most successful British costume drama series since the 1981 television serial of *Brideshead Revisited.*

By the third series, it had become one of the most widely watched television shows in the world. My question is WHY?? Why the fascination? Why such celebrity? We need to pause and take a closer look.

With a "long thoughtful look" can we begin to see something of God's message here in this TV show? Has the Holy Spirit been at work in the hearts and minds of a generation using this parable of a rich and privileged family from the early 20th century? Why has this become the most widely watched TV series in the world?

Is Jesus speaking through this movie set and nudging people towards spiritual receptivity? Is this a TV series we can comment on and in turn lead people back to an authentic relationship with Jesus Christ the author of real life? Can we use this TV show to stir the passions of a generation to live for Jesus? Is there a nudge in this TV show that may lead people towards spiritual receptivity?

By the way; what does a nudge look like? A nudge is a gentle push – a casual bump that gets your attention but doesn't really do any harm. A gentle nudge – pushes people in a direction – it gets you interested – it's a small jolt to stir awareness in a subject. It's a bit of a spiritual teaser to get your eyes and heart attuned to something stirring somewhere inside you. It's a gentle push in the right direction.

Matthew 13: 10 - 17 say this: "The disciples came up and asked, "Why do you tell stories?" He replied, "You've been given insight into God's kingdom. You know how it works. Not everybody has this gift, this insight; it hasn't been given to them. Whenever someone has a ready heart for this, the insights and understandings flow freely. But if there is no readiness, any trace of receptivity soon disappears. That's why I tell stories: to create readiness, to nudge the people toward receptive insight. In their present state they can stare till doomsday and not see it, listen till they're blue in the face and not get it."

Plain View

He continues; "I don't want Isaiah's forecast repeated all over again: 'Your ears are open but you don't hear a thing. Your eyes are awake but you don't see a thing. The people are blockheads! They stick their fingers in their ears so they won't have to listen; They screw their eyes shut so they won't have to look, so they won't have to deal with me face-to-face and let me heal them.' But you [speaking to His disciples] you have God-blessed eyes—eyes that see! And God-blessed ears—ears that hear! A lot of people, prophets and humble believers among them, would have given anything to see what you are seeing, to hear what you are hearing, but never had the chance."

What were the disciple's eyes seeing? What were the disciple's ears hearing? The answer is Jesus - they were seeing and hearing Him as Messiah. He was standing right before them and speaking - they touched Him - they ate with Him and they ministered with Him. They had God-blessed ears and God-blessed eyes.

Others were blockheads - they stick their fingers in their ears and screw shut their eyes so they won't have to look. The group of people who were looking for the Messiah were the ones who missed His coming. The religious rulers of His day weren't hearing and weren't seeing! AMAZING!!

Jesus says that people do this "so they won't have to deal with me face to face and let me heal them!" We all know there is a cost to count when we decide to follow Jesus - but the rewards are eternal!

Here is my foundation; is it possible that we can work with the Holy Spirit in nudging people towards spiritual receptivity? Can we identify the secular prophets in popular culture and give them voice? Can we turn people to the "Unknown God" like Paul did in Acts 17 and grab their attention leading them towards spiritual reality?

Can we at least get a conversation started? Can we, through popular stories on TV, create a readiness in the hearts of people to see and hear the truth about Jesus? Can we encourage them to open their eyes and ears and see Jesus face to face, to deal with the spiritual reality of Christ and be healed?

Downton Abbey is a great story - well produced - the actors are brilliant in their craft - this is a well-made TV series and as a result it has a loyal following across the world. There's a sense of excellence about this show - nothing shoddy here - everything is top class.

But *Downton Abbey* is a show that stirs up emotions within us; very deep emotions some almost inarticulate to the human spirit.

- The past seems so much more palatable – pleasant – agreeable.
- The charmed lives of this aristocratic family stir a sense of privilege in our own broken hearts.
- We wish we could live their lives because they look so much better than our own lives and our own reality.
- It stirs a desire within us that makes us think we were "made for another world".

Let's face it though - the past seems simpler and easier for us to navigate – it's a known quantity. There's something within each of us that desires to hearken back to the good old days.

As a pastor for 40 years I see it all the time - if you've been a Christian for more than 10 years - the old songs are the best songs - the old way of doing it is the best way of doing it - we try to relive those glory days as if they were the best days ever! Even Jesus said the old wine is better! Check out Luke 5:39.

My advice is to take off your rose tinted glasses, give them a wipe and get a life. The past is gone and the future is before us. Let's make our future bright by making good decisions today! The best is yet to come. Don't long for the past - it's gone and we can never re-live it! We all love a good yarn – we love an intricate story that gets us in – that gets our interest week by week. The nature of an hour TV show once a week gets us ready for our favourite character. We love the feeling of outrage when someone acts in an inappropriate manner and we love to hate the bad guys who scheme. We love the seditious behaviour of those nasty servants! We love a plot that unfolds and we get to be taken by surprise.

This of course has nothing to do with our own lives and routines, hey? This has nothing to do with our schedules, nappy changes, washing, boring job routines - hey? It's okay - TV shows like this provide escape - it's called entertainment. We all love to be entertained.

The lifestyles of the rich and famous are attractive to us. They stir our imagination. We think how good it would be to live in that house with servants and dinner at 8 wearing tuxedoes and fashionable dresses. How delightful it would be for us to be served by others. We'd love to wake to a cooked breakfast every morning served by the maids and all we need to do is ask for more coffee please James! We are tempted to imagine ourselves in that big house with cooks, waiters, chauffer, maids who make the beds, wash the dishes, clean up the kitchen, wash the cloths and clean the house – oh and polishing the silver.

As we imagine this kind of lifestyle we get a bit of escape for the drudgery of our own reality – we can vicariously live our lives through the life of our favourite character. There's nothing wrong with a bit of entertainment, hey?

TV shows like *Downton Abbey* reveal and expose the horror of the hole carved inside of each and every one of us. TV shows like *Downton Abbey* open up wounds and stirs up secret desires that we can safely fulfil simply by watching someone else's life. We all secretly wish we could live like that.

This is, by the way, the same emotions that stir when we buy a lottery ticket or hear about the people who win big. This is the same emotion that says we need a bigger car, a bigger house, more clothes or more children. We believe we were "made for another world" and will seek to do anything we can to get that reality. We're disappointed, even disillusioned, when we don't get what we think we deserve.

By the way - it is this desire that remains unfulfilled that leads us to abandon our dreams and live the life of the status quo - thriving off mediocrity and prospering in our apathy. We get depressed - become negative and lose perspective on real life - we become cynics putting down ambition in others because we have failed to make it to that other world. We lose our drive for the dreams God places in our lives and we miss out on our destiny.

We watch shows like *Downton Abbey* – we see a more civilized microcosm of a family's life. We see the genteel way the women are wooed by the appropriate suitors. We watch and long for a more noble way to live and love. The weddings are from another world. Even the scandal is underplayed when compared to today! When someone dies you'll never be subject to a CSI autopsy room!

We watch *Downton Abbey* and at times we ache over our own devastations; our own loss. We watch and hope there will be a balm or salve that will take away the pain of own mistakes. We watch and for an hour we can repress our own regrets and get a glimpse of a better life, a more noble life and a more genteel way of living. Maybe this is why entertainment is so therapeutic to a broken soul.

A show of this kind releases us for an hour from the drudgery of our trapped life and we feel free for a while. These are the same feelings when women read *Mills and Boon* love stories. There's a wish a desire and ache for a strong manly man to come and woo you, to desire you, and love you in a way that will make you fulfilled and content.

Standing in plain view today I see Jesus. I can see His Holy Spirit working through TV shows like *Downton Abbey*. If I take the time to look a little closer I can see the Holy Spirit using shows like *Downton*

Abbey to stir eternity in the hearts of some who are connecting with this show.

I can see just how Jesus is using these stories to nudge people towards spiritual receptivity – stirring a desire for insight, fulfilment and a sense of purpose. We switch off the telly with a sense of wellbeing but, like Chinese food, an hour later we have this unfulfilled ache of human hunger, yearning and desire. We were made for another world.

Questions and desires abound – some questions and desires are articulated but most are not. Most of the questions and desires are haunting thoughts we find difficult to express. Many of the emotions we feel during the hour long TV shows are dark, deep, vague, evocative and unclear. We're let bereft, lost, disoriented and confused longing for another fix in a week's time.

Why can't I live this kind of noble life?
Why can't I be wealthy like those people?
Why am I always scratching around for another pound to pay the bills?
Why don't I have a family like this?
Where was my father when I needed him?
Why won't my mother love me like she loves her daughters?
Why can't I be happy, beautiful and pampered?
Why can't I have social skills and graces like them?
Where is God?

The danger is we turn off the TV and are brutally confronted by our reality. Life seems boring, too hard, filled with too many detours and trials. The reality of life crowds us in and we feel like we've become claustrophobic, strangled by our reality, our debt, our struggles, our jobs, our friends, our flat, our school, our own sense of hopelessness – living this life with no sense of drive, no direction, no obvious purpose – we get bored - depressed – we become unmotivated – there's no sense of destiny.

We live passionless lives, we feel trivialised and confused by the cold hardness of reality. We feel lost and alone in a huge universe that has no edges.

Jesus said in **John 14: 1-3** "Do not let your hearts be troubled. You believe in God; ***believe also in me***. My Father's house has many rooms; if that were not so, would I have told you that I am going there to prepare a place for you? And if I go and prepare a place for you, I will come back and take you to be with me that you also may be where I am."

In my Father's house there are many rooms! You believe in God, believe also in me - these are the words of Jesus. Have faith in Christ - our future is assured.

Here's the truth - ***you were made for another world!***

We were created to walk with God in this life and live with God forever in Heaven. God is meant to satisfy our soul. God is meant to bring fulfilment to our lives. God brings meaning to our existence here on earth. God brings purpose to my job, my marriage, and my friendships. God is the source of my passion. My connection with Jesus defines me not my possessions, not my house and not my money. My hope is built on nothing less than Jesus' blood and righteousness.

Even in this world - the words of Jesus inspire us! Do not let your heart be troubled - if you have faith in me then you will be able to navigate this world with all of its difficulties and know my peace in your hearts.

If we have Jesus filling the hole of eternity - if He comes to live in that gaping hole within us then we will experience a level of fulfilment that only God can provide!

Plain View

The hole in our hearts created by God can only be filled by God. Staying fulfilled, staying satisfied - living with purpose - living with passion - walking in our destiny is all part of staying connected with Jesus Christ in this life!

Jesus Christ: Radical beyond measure

Part Five: Elvis Sightings - Seeing Jesus Christ in some Remarkable Places

*When he was at the table with them, he took bread, gave thanks, broke it and began to give it to them. Then their eyes were opened **and they recognised him**, and he disappeared from their sight. **Luke 24:30-31** (Emphasis added.)*

*They came to Philip, who was from Bethsaida in Galilee, with a request. "Sir," they said, "we would like to see Jesus. **John 12:21***

Elvis sighting quote:
"I saw Elvis in a leather tannery (undisclosed location to protect the King's privacy, of course) eating Chester Fried Chicken and drinking a Yahoo in the break room at lunch. Of course I knew immediately who this great icon was by the groovy burns that would make Greg Brady lay down in fetal position and weep. I spoke with him briefly, not letting on that of course I know this is Elvis, about the global economy and how it had affected the leather industry but I think he was more concerned with the lack of donut delivery service in the area, "What's with all the Dunkin Donuts in the area and I can't get any delivered?" was the quote I'll always remember. Overall, the King looked good for his age despite the polyester he was wearing. LONG LIVE THE KING!!!!"

Chapter 19: Conclusions

In the onslaught of the twenty first century pre-Christian atmosphere our eyes become unfocused, almost distracted from the rich tapestry of Jesus sightings.

We have been tempted to become legalists; criticising, condemning and censuring every movie, song or TV show that young people are watching. We do this with a sense of misguided concern. But the Holy Spirit has not abandoned popular culture. Indeed, He has embedded Himself there like a foreign correspondent for us to find Him and reveal Jesus to the waiting world.

You'd *expect* to see Jesus in the scriptures but are we on the lookout for the unmistakable DNA of Christ in the world? Like a watermark, for those with eyes to see, His person can be observed on the pages of twenty first century life. Hello! To be honest He's in plain view. His big sticky finger prints have been discovered all over modern culture; we've put them through IAFIS and found out they belonged to Jesus Christ! The forensic evidence of His presence is obvious; He's been here and some of us didn't recognise Him.

Common grace takes a bow as we watch Jesus on the red carpets of the world's film ceremonies. Like the experience of Paul on Mars Hill, the Holy Spirit has gone before us to help a generation with no Christian background or understanding come to faith in Christ.

If we can discover the switches to flip in this crowded and complex media saturated world, we can kick start the eternal hardwiring which exists inside of every person on the planet.

One glimpse of the eternal Christ in pop culture could lead us back to an exposition of scripture that will shatter the unbelieving heart and lead to conversion, repentance and a salvation no one could have expected. We need to be "wise as serpents"[135], aware and open, constantly on the lookout; taking a closer look at everything around us - searching and probing.

Hebrews 2:7-9 says "You made him a little lower than the angels; you crowned him with glory and honour and put everything under his feet." In putting everything under Him, God left nothing that is not subject to him. Yet at present we do not see everything subject to him. ***But we see Jesus...***

From Genesis through to the book of Revelation you'll find Jesus. Through the sacred writings, as well as through creation, cultures and modern societies, there runs a crimson thread of redemption. For those with an eye to see, you will find a picture of Jesus on almost every page of scripture and littered through the pages of history.

---

[135] Matthew 10:16

Plain View

Listen; this was the great desire of the ages - for God to reveal Himself in His Son! This was a plan set in motion from before time began. It was a plan so audacious it was first developed within the confines of eternity and contained only in Divinity's mind. It was a plan no one but Deity would have instigated or even conceived. It was a plan that only God could have prompted. The plan was to make known, Him who is Father of eternity and Prince of Peace. It was a plan to reveal Jesus in all of His glory and wonder.

Though the scriptures give us a full, detailed and fairly extensive pictures of Jesus Christ, we will one day understand how limited even this revelation is. There is coming a day where though we have heard of Him by the hearing of the ear, we will see Him face to face and live![136]

Throughout the Bible we get a glimpse of His majesty. The Old Testament shows Him off in shadows but the New Testament allows us such a foretaste of glory so as to make us want to fall before Him in abandon. There is a day coming when we will see Him high and lifted up and His garments will fill the heavenly Temple[137], our resurrected and heavenly minds will once again burst with understanding and yet still hunger for more.

We have eternity as our backdrop for gaining even more insight and more appreciation of His absolute matchless personality. In this earthly dwelling we see as through a glass darkly but there will be a day when we will see clearly and realise our knowledge and comprehension of who He is will continue to expand through eternity. Even with the myriad of superlatives in language, we'll always struggle to describe Him!

In every book of the Bible we see Jesus Christ; He is the watermark on every page, He is the logo imprint. His character and personality

---

[136] Job 42:5
[137] Isaiah 6:1

go into the branding of this book of books. To some He is invisible, but to others... we see Him in sublime glory!

In Genesis, Jesus is the seed of woman who crushes the head of that old Serpent at the cost of a bruising of His own heal. Jesus is seen in the sacrifice of animals whose blood was shed and their skins used to cover the naked bodies of both Adam and Eve. Jesus is heard as Abel cries out after his murder. Jesus is seen in the building of Noah's Ark; He is our salvation. Jesus is seen in the rainbow after the flood; He is the promise of grace.

Jesus is seen in every book of the Bible; He is Abraham's shield and very great reward. Jesus is seen in the appearance of Melchizedek, king of Salem "king of righteousness and king of peace!"[138] Jesus is seen in the sacrifice of Isaac, the promised son to Abraham. Jesus is the ram caught in the thicket.

Jesus is seen on every page of scripture. He is the centre of God's plans for the universe; this plan is from before the moment of creation, hidden in eternity to the day when the Earth will be burnt with fire and time will be no more. There never has been a time and there never will be a time when Jesus is not central, predominant and sovereign to all that is, or will be around us. It is impossible for Him to be peripheral, secondary or marginal; He is and will always be the greatest phenomenon that has ever crossed the horizons of this world.

If eternity had a beginning, He is the Father of Eternity; the progenitor of time. He is the creator of and Lord of Time. He is the fabric and foundation of space. He lives and exists unaffected by the ages, unaltered by seasons and unchanged by eras and epochs. He is impervious to the hours that pass, untouched by the changing of a calendar and changeless in nature.

---

[138] Hebrews 7:2

Jesus existed before He was born in Bethlehem. As it says so majestically in John's gospel: "In the beginning was the Word and the Word was with God and the Word was God. He was with God in the beginning." He declares in **John 8:58**, "'I tell you the truth,' Jesus answered, 'before Abraham was born, I am!'"

He was the author of the beginning; He was the "Imagin-ator" of time. He is the Alpha and the Omega. He represents the creativity of the ages; He is the inspiration for the very concept of the aeons. From the depths of the ever increasing Universe to the tiniest sub-atomic particle... He is the creator of Time and Space.

He is the Sovereign One whose very fullness fills everything in every way.[139] It stretches and warps the mind of those with puny human brains when they seek to understand the concept of "His fullness." It disturbs the equilibrium of all life when we seek to understand the fact that "all of God is everywhere" and there is no place on Earth from which we escape His pervading presences.[140] Our brains break, our imaginations are exhausted and our deliberations divinely twisted when we consider the ubiquitous saturation of His being. Jesus is very BIG – unimaginably SUBSTANTIAL.

When we consider His knowledge, we cry out with Job; "Can anyone teach knowledge to God, since he judges even the highest?"[141]

Nothing is hidden from Him[142]. The mind of Deity has no limitation as we would understand limitations. We are fully known.[143] Every aspect of, not just us as unique individuals, but every aspect of mankind is known to Jesus because He created us. There is no strain of DNA which God did not foresee and fully know; there is no finger print in all the ages of the world He did not manufacture from

---

[139] Ephesians 1: 23
[140] Psalms 139: 7
[141] Job 21:22
[142] Hebrews 4:13
[143] 1 Corinthians 13:12

scratch. The length and breadth of His knowing can never be defined, classified or demarcated by the human ethos.

Written in a billion skies...
As we look to the depths of space and see galaxies, universes and the countless stars; we behold His power. When we look at the order of the human body with its complexities and the intricacies, we gaze upon sheer genius and absolute brilliance. His creative capacity is matchless.

There is none who could come close to compare with Him.[144] From the furthest corner of space, trillions of light years from our own planet to the tiniest speck of dust on a book; we see the incredible, indescribable and inconceivable supremacy of Jesus.

His control and influence is beyond our description. He is astonishing and staggering in His omnipotence. Jesus is Almighty,[145] He is limitless in His power, His strength, His energy and His might. There is nothing impossible for God.[146]

Jesus Christ represents to us not only as the centrepiece of civilization as we know it, but is the focus and main attraction of all that is or that is to come. He shares the spot light with no one; He is the focus of all creation and all that *is* finds its place in Him. He is the Designer of all we see. His creativity still flows in the Earth and through the farthest heavens. He is remarkable, original and thoroughly one of a kind, someone who continues to create so we can behold His glory, His wisdom and His power.

Jesus Christ has centre stage. He is unparalleled, He is unprecedented and He represents the distinguished ideas of what

---

[144] Psalms 89:6
[145] Revelation 4:8
[146] Luke 1:37

Plain View

mankind can conceive or possibly create. He has no rivals and no equals.

He has remained the most inspirational personality to the song writers, philosophers and poets of our world. He is the most complex thought to the academic.

He remains the foundational truth of Christian doctrine and He remains the Way, the Truth and the Life[147]; a light to all the world throughout every age.

No one who has ever walked this planet has been more qualified to be the all sufficient saviour to a world lost in sin and brokenness. No one has ever, from since time began, become the sole survivor of God's anger and still lives to tell His story. No one has ever taken the full force of God's judgement and survived to bring salvation to a world so shattered. All of God's anger was poured out upon Him and He withstood it all because he died for others, not for His own sin.

Jesus Christ was the Lamb of God.[148] Jesus was the supreme sacrifice for the sins of the world. No one had ever qualified for this role in the history of the world. Deep within His humanity, the knowledge resided that He was "the Lamb slain",[149] His blood would be shed so that others would know peace with God.

Jesus Christ is seen in shadow as Jacob's ladder, He is seen in the Passover Lamb, He stands as Joshua's Captain of the Lord's Host, He is heard when Israel shouts at Jericho's wall. Jesus Christ is seen in shadow as the ministry of the High Priest; and you see Him as the great Prophets who speak in the name of the Lord and in shadow you see Him in every solemn sacrifice called upon by Israel to perform. His shadow is seen in the words of the prophet Isaiah when he said

---

[147] John 14:6
[148] John 1:29
[149] Revelation 5:9

a Virgin will be found with child.[150] We see Him in the tears of Jeremiah as he weeps for a city being destroyed.

Every special feast day and festival celebrated by Israel is a shadow of Jesus Christ. Even the Law delivered to Moses was a shadow of Jesus Christ to come. "The law is only a shadow of the good things that are coming not the realities themselves." **Hebrews 10:1**

Colossians 2:17 says this about the shadows; "These are a shadow of the things that were to come; the reality, however, is found in Christ." We now no longer need a shadow; we have Jesus Christ. This becomes our responsibility and great joy to reveal Him to a waiting world.

Hebrews 1:1-3 says "In the past God spoke to our forefathers through the prophets at many times and in various ways, but in these last days he has spoken to us by his Son, whom he appointed heir of all things, and through whom he made the universe. The Son is the radiance of God's glory and the exact representation of his being, sustaining all things by his powerful word. After he had provided purification for sins, he sat down at the right hand of the Majesty in heaven." God has spoken to us through Jesus Christ who declares that He is the Son of God and the Son of Man.

It is Jesus who is heir of all things, Jesus who is the creator of the universe, Jesus who appears as the exact radiance of all of God's glory and it is Jesus who is the precise representation of His Being, His essence, His character and His Nature.

It is Jesus Christ who sustains all things by His power and it is Jesus Christ who sits at the right hand of the Majesty in Heaven. Jesus emerges on to the screen of time to reveal Himself. Jesus is the same yesterday, today and forever!!

---

[150] Isaiah 7:14

Plain View

The Holy Spirit, whose main work is to glorify Jesus, is moving powerfully on those who seek to exalt Christ.

The Spirit of Christ has not left us bereft; we are not orphans. The Holy Spirit of Christ has gone before us to invade time and space. The Holy Spirit of Christ has left indelible finger prints all over this world. With eternity in the hearts of man, Jesus Christ by His Spirit has left behind so much forensic evidence of His activity, it is impossible for us to not see Him.

Jesus said, "If I be lifted up I will draw all men unto myself."
Our work is to lift up Jesus Christ for all to see.

- Jesus Christ is matchless in grace, mercy and kindness.
- He is LOVE and explains what love is by loving us while we were yet sinners.
- He is gentle but He is also a King – a king of righteousness, King of Kings and Lord of Lords.
- He is the ruler of all the kings of the Earth and there is no power in Heaven or Earth that can defeat Him. He has no equals and there are none to rivals His rule.
- He is the Almighty; He is the King of Heaven, the King of glory and King of all the ages.
- Jesus Christ is Sovereign; He rules, He reigns and He is supreme; there is no limit to His power.
- There is no limit to His love or His grace – there is no human measurement to determine His love, there is no measurement to ascertain either the heights or the depth of His concern for us.

He is strength itself. He is sincere – totally without wax – not *one* of His actions is ever artificial or lacking in earnestness. He will never waver or hesitate in His love; He is steadfast, resolute and unswerving in His commitment to our best.

He is graceful and never seeks to embarrass us, taking seriously the dignity of every human being on Earth. He is impartial in His compassion. Kindness, sympathy and benevolence are found in His touch. He rushes to show mercy beyond what is humanly possible because he is GOD!

He is the most outstanding person to ever grace this Earth. He is Hope, He is Faith and He is the desire of all ages. Civilization has never before seen such a man as He; this world has never envisaged such a saviour.

Unparalleled and unprecedented is our Lord Jesus Christ. No one has a name like His; He is exalted; high and lifted up. At the very sound of His name demons tremble, sins are forgiven and all things are made new!

His blood is able to cleanse the worst of sin's stains. His blood can make the vilest sinner whole, and through faith in His blood, He becomes the atonement, the perfect sacrifice for the sins of all the world. In His blood is justice. In His blood there is redemption. We have been justified by the shedding of His blood. Through the shedding of His blood we have peace with God, we've been reconciled with God. By His blood the anger and judgement of God has been satisfied. His blood has brought us near, once again, to the heart of God.

His blood is the blood of a New Covenant between God and man. Jesus Christ, through the shedding of His blood, has become the mediator of a new and better agreement with God. His blood has purchased men for God!

Jesus Christ is unmatched, beyond compare and without equal in Heaven, on the Earth and under the Earth. Yet He is a man just like us. He was tempted in all ways, yet without sin. He is a high priest who is able to sympathise with our every weakness – could there ever be one to rival Him?

David cries out in **Psalms 86:8**, "Among the gods there is none like you, O Lord; no deeds can compare with yours."

As our intercessor, He is able to supply strength to the weary; he is there when we are tempted and supports us. Jesus Christ is able to sustain us in times of trial, give us victory when we are attacked and He encourages us to be "of good cheer" when we encounter troubles because He has overcome the world.

By His Spirit who lives within us, He is able to give guidance. He is able to guard all that we have committed to Him. By the same Spirit who raised Jesus Christ from the dead, we are quickened and made alive in Him. His Spirit, the Spirit of Christ, leads and guides into all truth, brings back to our remembrance the things he said and is able to build us up as we pray in the Spirit.

The very source of power which was present at creation lives within us and is *active* within us; this power quickens us! For those who call Him "Saviour" and "Lord" we are indwelt by Jesus Christ; His Spirit lives within us. There is a fresh supply of the anointing for each of us every day because the Spirit of Christ lives within us.

His burden is light and His yoke is easy; as we work together in harmony with Jesus Christ we will experience His passion, His enthusiasm and His zeal for all the things concerning His Kingdom.

Jesus Christ is supernatural, miraculous and very potent. He has authority over demons, He can heal the sick, raise the dead and perform miracles. The greatest miracle in the entire universe Jesus performs is when anyone calls upon His name.

We are saved when we ask Him to come and live within us. Salvation remains the greatest of miracles upon the Earth; all other supernatural activity flows from this very act we call salvation. Power, a million times over, is released when just ONE sinner repents and accepts Jesus and His salvation. Angels are so amazed with the act of salvation that they watch on in absolute amazement.[151]

So strong, so all-encompassing is this impact of Christ's saving grace upon a person's life the Bible says we become "new creations." The old is taken away behold all things become new.[152]

My sin is washed away, my conscience is cleaned and my future is secure and all because of Jesus living in me. And when he comes to live within me, the powers of darkness are broken over my life. The force of the Devil and every evil spirit is defeated because of Jesus Christ's death and resurrection.

Paul powerfully confirms this in **Colossians 1:13-14**; "For he has rescued us from the dominion of darkness and brought us into the kingdom of the Son he loves, in whom we have redemption, the forgiveness of sins."

Jesus Christ sets the prisoners free, delivers those in bondage to sin or Satan. Every curse is broken and every power of evil over us has been destroyed! Jesus Christ breaks the chains of cancelled sin and we are no longer walking under the prince of the power of the air[153] but live under the anointing of God and walk in the power of the Spirit of Christ.

"Jesus loves me this I know for the Bible tells me so!" [154]

Jesus defends the weak and the frail; He is a strong tower for those who are vulnerable. He loves children and desires to bless them, give them a destiny and a future hope. Those who are the under privileged, He reaches out to with understanding. He extends His concern to the poor and the broken, they are His special concern. He

---

[151] 1 Peter 1:12
[152] 2 Corinthians 5:17
[153] Ephesians 2:2
[154] Hymn by William Bradbury (1860)

Plain View

loves the needy and seeks justice for those in poverty, want and lack. He is with those who struggle. He loves the old and respects those who are advanced in years; He is a champion for the rights of women and treats them all with dignity, regardless of what past they may have had.

"Blessed are the poor in spirit, for theirs is the kingdom of Heaven. Blessed are those who mourn, for they will be comforted. Blessed are the meek, for they will inherit the Earth. Blessed are those who hunger and thirst for righteousness, for they will be filled. Blessed are the merciful, for they will be shown mercy. Blessed are the pure in heart, for they will see God. Blessed are the peacemakers, for they will be called sons of God."[155]

Jesus Christ is truly irresistible; few can resist Him for long. His appeal has lasted through the ages. He is overwhelming, compelling, and totally uncontainable. He is the lover of our soul, His grace is sufficient; and His mercies are new every morning. He is beautiful beyond description. He is our strong tower we can run into. He is a refuge and a present help in times of trouble. The Lord is my shepherd.

The Lord is my rock and my salvation, whom shall I fear?[156] Jesus Christ is the same yesterday today and forever.[157] He is our wisdom. He is our saviour. Jesus Christ is the Son of God and the Son of Man. Jesus is the Christ, the Messiah has come!

Jesus Christ is radical beyond measure. He is a dangerous Messiah. He is unstoppable! He is wild and at times unpredictable. He is a revolutionary of the highest order. He is indescribable. He is incomprehensible. Death had no chance of holding Him captive and the grave could not keep Him caged. He is King and Lord overall and

---

[155] Matthew 5:3-9
[156] Psalm 27 (paraphrase)
[157] Hebrews 13:8

he has defeated every power of darkness against us, defeated every enemy and reigns invincible forever.

"Worship God! For the testimony of Jesus is the spirit of prophecy." **Revelation 19:10**

Jesus Christ is irresistible; radical beyond measure!

Acknowledgements:

Nobody does this alone. So I would like to thank a lot of people for editing, reading and commenting on my book.

Editing is a hard, time consuming part of being an author. I want to thank a few people. Thank you to James Marlow, Tudor Howell, Patricia DeWitt, Owen Morgan, Gemma Neill, Phil Temple, Ian Currie, Lindsay Bruce, Paul Hilton and Pat French.

Thanks to Tim Handley for helping to make this book a possibility. You were a vital link in getting this book into print. Thanks so much for your efforts.

Thanks to Liz Morgan for working on my cover picture. You're creative, insightful and very professional in all you do.

Thanks to Denise Rawls for allowing me the countless hours to write this book. Couldn't have done it without you.